Ritual & Diplomacy

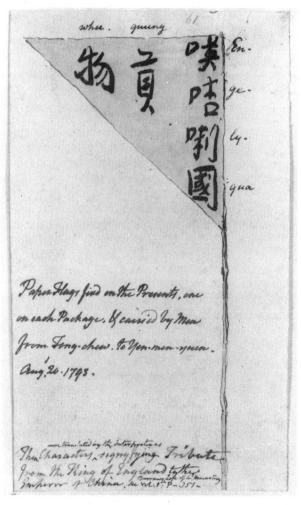

William Alexander's sketch of the flags attached to the gifts carried by the mission from George III to the Qianlong emperor. In fact, the characters state that the presents are 'English tribute articles'.
(Reproduced courtesy of the British Library, Oriental and India Office Collections, Alexander MSS.)

RITUAL & DIPLOMACY

The Macartney Mission to China
1792–1794

Papers Presented at the 1992 Conference of the
BRITISH ASSOCIATION FOR CHINESE STUDIES
Marking the Bicentenary of the
Macartney Mission to China

Edited by ROBERT A. BICKERS

THE BRITISH ASSOCIATION FOR CHINESE STUDIES
wellsweep

The British Association for Chinese Studies gratefully acknowledges the support of the UNIVERSITIES CHINA COMMITTEE and the BRITISH TAIWAN CULTURAL CENTRE in assisting with the publication of these papers.

First published in 1993
as a supplement to the *Bulletin of the British Association for Chinese Studies* by
THE BRITISH ASSOCIATION FOR CHINESE STUDIES
The Secretary, BACS
c/o The Great Britain-China Centre
15 Belgrave Square
London SW1X 8PS

in association with
THE WELLSWEEP PRESS
1 Grove End House
150 Highgate Road
London NW5 1PD

Represented & Distributed in the UK & Europe by:
PASSWORD (BOOKS) LTD
serving independent literary publishers in the United Kingdom
24 New Mount Street
Manchester M4 4DE

0 948454 19 9 paperback

BRITISH LIBRARY CATALOGUING-IN-PUBLICATION DATA
A catalogue record for this book is available from the British Library.

Designed and typeset by *wellsweep*
Printed and bound by E & E Plumridge

CONTENTS

INTRODUCTION

ROBERT A. BICKERS

THE CIRCUS OF ACADEMIC AND MEDIA CELEBRATION has been slowly girding itself up to mark the two hundredth anniversary of the arrival in China in 1793 of the first formal British diplomatic mission to that country. New narratives of the event have been published and an exhibition of sketches and other materials held at the British Museum, while a conference is due to be held in Beijing in 1993. As its contribution to this process the British Association for Chinese Studies convened a conference which inadvertently, but in retrospect rather pointedly, celebrated Lord Macartney's *departure* for China from Portsmouth on the 26th of September, 1792. Pointedly because the question of departures is a useful underlying theme, and one which characterised the papers presented and the discussions which accompanied them.

It is clear that we are still at the departure stage of the work that has begun and that can still be done to explicate and assess this symbolically resonant mission, although the ground breaking works of J. L. Cranmer-Byng and E. H. Pritchard alerted us to most of the pertinent material and debates about what actually happened.[1] The recent monographs of Alain Peyrefitte and Aubrey Singer both draw respectably on the large amounts of archival and printed material that survive, although both are biased towards the Western sources.[2] It was a mission quite notable for the writings its members left behind (and, of course, for the vivid sketches and water colours of William Alexander) and the public debate and interest it generated. From Sir George Staunton's *An Authentic Account of an Embassy from the King of Great Britain to the Emperor of China* onwards the bulk of accounts have been narratives or else based heavily on individual memoirs of the mission.

[1] See, for example, E. H. Pritchard, *The Crucial Years of Anglo-Chinese Relations 1750–1800*, Research Studies of the State College of Washington 4:3–4 (Pullman, Washington, 1936); J. L. Cranmer-Byng, *An Embassy to China: Being the journal kept by Lord Macartney during his embassy to the Emperor Ch'ien-lung 1793–1794* (London, 1962) and his 'Lord Macartney's Embassy to Peking in 1793 from Official Chinese Documents', *Journal of Oriental Studies*, 4:1–2 (1957–1958), pp. 117–87.
[2] Aubrey Singer, *The Lion and the Dragon: The Story of the First British Embassy to the Court of the Emperor Qianlong in Peking, 1792–1794* (London, 1992); Alain Peyrefitte, *L'empire immobile ou le choc des mondes* (Paris, 1989) translated as *The Collision of Two Civilisations: The British Expedition to China in 1792–4* (London, 1993).

The story might, then, appear to be already well told but in a telling recent note Harriet Zurndorfer has warned against seduction by the plethora of narratives, contemporary to the mission or modern.[1] The mission lends itself conveniently to symbolism and to reduction — the high hopes of the enterprise, the long slow journey to China and then to Peking and Jehol, the problem of the *koutou*, the mutual misunderstandings, the Qing court's dismissal of the British gifts, the infamous Qianlong edict to George III that noted his 'sincere humility and obedience', the slow journey home to report failure — these events and themes clearly suggest a framework for their telling, but one that is, as Zurndorfer noted, superficial. Both of Peyrefitte's choice of titles sum up the complacent structure of explication which the mission is too easily, and too often, forced into: a 'collision of civilisations', one of which is 'immobile' and the other, by implication, dynamic. A major problem here, of course, is that neither Singer nor Peyrefitte read Chinese and the assistance both have received with the Chinese documentation is ultimately no substitute. As a result such misleading generalisations, largely based on the British sources, and eighteenth century attitudes, continue to be perpetuated. It is clear that the fear of narration apparently evinced by professional historians has, so far, undoubtedly worked against a definitive exposition of the episode.

The present collection does not pretend to offer a definitive response. In fact, the resonance of the struggle over the *koutou*, the themes suggested by the Qianlong edict, and the question of the gifts brought by the British are important and fertile topics perhaps ill-suited to narration. These papers do, however, point out the range of themes being investigated (and also the range of sources in both languages being used) and suggest the ways in which they are being drawn out. P. J. Marshall first sketches out the background to the sending of the mission and sets it firmly in the context of domestic and East India Company politics. An explanation of British expectations of the mission and the behaviour of those sent is impossible without an understanding of the characters of the eighteenth century Britons involved, which he supplies. Zhang Shunhong broadens out his earlier work on the views of China to be found in the writings of members of the Macartney and Amherst missions[2] to look at the Qing Court's perceptions of the embassy and gives an assessment of some of the problems and reasons for the mission's failure. Wang Tseng-tsai contributes a sum-

[1] Harriet T. Zurndorfer, 'La sinologie immobile', *Etudes Chinoises*, 8:2 (1989), pp. 99–120.

[2] See his unpublished 1990 University of London Ph. D. thesis 'British views on China during the time of the Embassies of Lord Macartney and Lord Amherst (1790–1820)'.

mary of the mutual misunderstandings which characterised the mission and its reception. This was a tremendously symbolic mission, one that has become more so since; James Hevia discusses the symbolism inherent in the questions of the *koutou*, the mission's gifts and the famous Qianlong letter to George III, and its place in conceptions of the history of Sino-Western relations. My own paper deals more broadly with the role of myths and interpretations of history in British treaty port society in the early 20th century to which the Macartney episode contributed.

It is clear then, that there is still more work to be done about the mission, its context, its written and visual products, and its reverberations.[1] The papers collected here give an indication of the directions this work can move in and some of the themes which can be teased out to stimulating effect. It must never be forgotten, of course, that this was not the first failed putative ambassadorial mission to China from a European state. The two Dutch missions of the early seventeenth century had been even more humiliating for the participants.[2] They however, occurred at a time less retrospectively susceptible to the clichés of Chinese stagnation and cultural collision. The better known theatricality of the Macartney mission, its contemporary publicity, and its historiographical importance, continue to draw our attention to it, and rightly so. It does not need to be debunked, or belittled, but it does need to be properly written up, and rightly set in its context. These papers, and the researches they draw on, indicate the way this is being done.

It was perhaps also appropriate for the conference to mark this earlier date because it was not, after all, a successful mission by anybody's standards: not one of Macartney's stated aims was achieved and the tone of the discussions between the mission and the Qing court was often ill-tempered. On the voyage home Macartney described the mission as a 'tedious and painful employment'[3]. Despite the obvious advantages of the large body of knowledge gained about China and the Chinese[4] it was an expensive failure. Furthermore, the mission could be said to have marked the departure of

---

[1] One of the specific topics now being approached concerns the scientific objects taken by the mission, see, for example, Harriet T. Zurndorfer, 'Comment la science et la technologie se vendaient à la Chine au XVIIIe siècle', *Etudes Chinoises*, 7:2 (1988), pp. 59–90. For an indication of another avenue yet to be fully explored see the research in progress of Patrick Dransfield on the question of the acquisition of tea plants by the mission.

[2] See John Wills, *Embassies and Illusions: Dutch and Portuguese envoys to K'ang-hsi, 1666–1687* (Cambridge, Massachusetts, 1984).

[3] Cranmer-Byng, *Embassy to China*, p. 220.

[4] See, for example, Macartney's 'Observations on China', ibid., pp. 221–78.

relations between the British and the Qing empires into what were eventually unpleasant waters, marked by anniversaries little noted in this country.

The BACS conference held between September 28th and 30th 1992 at the School of Oriental and African Studies, and by implication these papers and this book, would not have been possible without the generous financial support of the following bodies: the British Academy, the British Council, the British Taiwan Cultural Institute and the Universities China Committee. Acknowledgements should also go to the Department of History of the School of Oriental Studies for funding a colloquium held after the conference in which some of the participants, together with other British historians, reviewed their findings and the state of research. Thanks should also go to Aubrey Singer for his constant encouragement of the entire project and for chairing some of the sessions. The present volume would not have been possible without the support of the British Taiwan Cultural Institute and the Universities China Committee. Thanks must also go to Frances Wood, head of the Chinese section at the British Library, Oriental and India Office Collections, for supplying the illustrations, which are taken from the sketchbooks of William Alexander.

BRITAIN AND CHINA IN THE LATE EIGHTEENTH CENTURY

P. J. MARSHALL

FOR HISTORIANS OF THE LONG EVOLUTION of Britain's relations with China the Macartney mission is like the beam of a searchlight, freezing into sudden illumination much that has been unfolding obscurely. In launching the embassy and in their instructions for it, British ministers, the East India Company and Macartney himself revealed their assumptions about China and their hopes for the future. A relatively small embassy produced a large volume of writing or visual representations: Macartney wrote dispatches and kept a journal, Sir George Staunton and John Barrow produced books, a valet and a private soldier also published their accounts and one of the expedition's scientists, Dr Gillan, recorded his observations. Thomas Hickey, the embassy's official 'painter' was not notably productive, but its 'draughtsman', William Alexander, brought home an extensive portfolio of drawings and other members of the expedition also drew Chinese scenes. Even thirteen-year old George Staunton recorded his impressions in a journal. Like all travel writing, the literary legacy of the embassy is of course not only a record of observation, but it is also a record of prior expectations and of contemporary accepted wisdom about China.

For most historians what the light provided by the mission is most likely to illuminate is a long-term shift in attitudes. Put very crudely, this is a shift from an inclination to Sino-philia in the late seventeenth or early eighteenth century with its admiration for an imagined China, to the disdain for the supposedly known China that was becoming an object for pressure and ultimately for the coercion of the opium wars. How does the late eighteenth century fit into this progression? I will try to argue that the evidence of the Macartney mission suggests that the shift is well under way by the 1790s. For most British people who had any concern with it, China was ceasing to be a world beyond the ordinary, capable of teaching lessons about government and the ordering of society or even of offering much in the way of exotic models for artistic improvisation. It was a place about which what was presumed to be exact knowledge was steadily accumulating. This knowledge enabled China's performance to be assessed by proven criteria thought to be applicable to all societies. These criteria generally found China seriously deficient in terms of government, scientific and technical achievement and in the standard of living it afforded its people. Even Chinoiserie had largely fallen out of fashion.

For British people, however they might envisage it, China was no longer by the eighteenth century merely a subject for curious speculation. The British and the Chinese empires were coming close to physical contact. The conquest of Bengal had brought British power up to the frontiers of Nepal, a state whose expansionist tendencies towards Tibet led to conflict with the Chinese. At the same time the enormous increase in the tea trade through Canton made China a very significant consideration in British commercial strategy. The mission was an attempt to establish regular diplomatic relations and to gain commercial concessions. Persuasion and appeals to mutual interest were to be the embassy's tactics. Macartney was, however, only the most eminent of those who recognised that concessions could be extracted by force. The use of force was not yet seriously on any British agenda: it seemed incompatible with Britain's major interests in China and in Macartney's case any recourse to forcible means was repugnant to his sense of 'reason' and 'humanity', 'whilst a ray of hope remains for succeeding by gentle ones.'[1] Nevertheless, what had been inconceivable had become thinkable: the fabulous had become the mundane and inhibitions about the use of force against recalcitrance that threatened British interests might not last.

The British had played very little part in the flow of information about China that reached Europe before the middle of the eighteenth century. The great body of this information came from the religious orders and above all from the Jesuits with their access to the imperial court at Peking. Jesuit accounts varied in their interpretation of China and were certainly not the unalloyed panegyrics on all things Chinese that they are sometimes taken to have been. The needs of the Jesuits' own conversion strategies, however, ensured that the overall thrust was to present China in a favourable light by European criteria. Confucianism embodied a set of doctrines based on reason and awareness of natural law. Chinese government followed rational principles to enhance the welfare of the people, applied by enlightened officials under an enlightened emperor. The people were obedient. A harmonious social order based on respect for age and authority prevailed throughout the empire. A huge population was busily employed in highly productive agriculture and in crafts whose matchless quality was above all shown in the manufacture of porcelain and textiles.

---

[1] *An Embassy to China: Lord Macartney's Journal 1793–4*, ed J. L. Cranmer-Byng, (London, 1961), p. 213.

Chinese objects were imported in increasing quantities into Europe, stimulated by a growing connoisseurship which was fed by 'export' items especially produced for the European market. What were assumed to be Chinese motifs were freely adapted to produce Chinoiserie effects in furniture, interior decoration, gardens and some buildings.

The British public seems to have shared in the general western European interest in things Chinese. Jesuit and other accounts were translated into English and discussions of China in British writings about the world generally endorsed Jesuit verdicts. The English East India Company were major importers of Chinaware in bulk, while the private trade of the officers of the Company's ships brought back higher quality goods, porcelain, paper hangings and small pieces of furniture. Chinoiserie took root in Britain in a considerable 'Japanning' or lacquer industry, in such artifacts as 'Chinese Chippendale', in Chambers' designs for Kew or in the remarkable effusion of Claydon House.

Perspectives on China were changing in Europe and Britain well before the dispatch of the Macartney mission. Most commentators have noted a change in tone around the middle of the eighteenth century. The authority of the Jesuits began to be treated with greater scepticism. Elements in their writings which implied criticism of Chinese civilisation are stressed and other hostile accounts, such as that of the author of Anson's *Voyage Round the World,* with its robust critique of China based on a visit to Canton, were given greater prominence. English literati of the mid-eighteenth century, such as Oliver Goldsmith, Samuel Johnson or Thomas Percy, adopted a generally questioning and carping tone in their treatment of Chinese topics. The Chinese taste went into something of an eclipse. European, including English, porcelain came to be preferred by many to imported Chinese ware. Chinese motifs had no standing in the dominant neo-classicism of the later eighteenth century.

Chinoiserie was a European invention suited to a Rococo taste for lightness and fancy which was waning by the 1750s; depictions of Chinese government and society based on Jesuit accounts were just as much European constructions to fulfil needs which were also passing by mid century. Qualities of stability combined with respect for tradition, order and hierarchy, which had been so appealing to Jesuits in the seventeenth century, no longer appealed to British intellectuals who were committed to ideals of progress and improvement. Much of the vogue for an enlightened China in an earlier period depended on the polemical uses to which it could be put, above all by Voltaire, as a counter example to political and ecclesiastical obscurantism in contemporary France. The English had always been less in need of counter examples and by the second half of the eighteenth century national self-confidence was at a very high ebb. The English were 'at this moment', Lord Macartney confided to his pocket book for the China voyage, 'the first people of the world — whenever they are out of their own country it is acknowledged. Their generosity, the child of opulence and industry, is unbounded and their good sense, the scholar of experience and relaxation [and] meditation have set them above the other nations who have not had so fair opportunities of exercising the one, and improving the other.'[1] 'It is no small advantage arising from the embassy', he concluded in his journal, 'that so many Englishmen have been seen at Pekin, from whose brilliant appearance and prudent demeanour a most favourable idea has been formed of the country which had sent them.'[2] If counter examples were sought in the late eighteenth century, they were far more likely to be alternatives embodying spontaneity of natural feelings rather than the over-polished, tightly regulated Chinese civilisation of the Jesuit tradition. The repression of spontaneity and naturalness became part of the European critique of Chinese society.

Not only were the messages that the Jesuits had transmitted about China no longer ones which Europeans necessarily wished to hear, but the value of the Jesuits as observers was also called into question. They lacked the detachment and 'scientific' exactness expected of the new wave of exploration, of which the Macartney mission was most emphatically a part. In his instructions Macartney was reminded that voyages 'at the public expense in the pursuit of knowledge and for the discovery and observation of distant countries and manners' were one of the glories of George III's reign.[3] Travel accounts of a previous age were now suspect. Adam Smith wrote of descriptions of Chinese public works, which were 'drawn up by weak and wondering travellers, frequently by stupid and lying missionaries. If they had been examined by more intelligent eyes ... they would not perhaps appear to be so wonderful.'[4] John Barrow commented that 'The voluminous communications of the missionaries are by no means satisfactory'.[5]

---

[1] Bodleian, MS Eng. Misc., f. 533, fol. 12.

[2] *Journal*, p. 214.

[3] *Chronicles of the East India Company Trading to China 1635–1834*, ed H. B. Morse, 5 vols. (Oxford, 1926–9), ii. 232.

[4] *Wealth of Nations*, eds R. H. Campbell and A. S. Skinner, 2 vols. (Oxford, 1976–9), ii. 729–30.

[5] *Travels in China*, 2nd edn. (London, 1806), p. 3.

The Jesuit accounts were regarded as deficient in two main respects. Somewhat unfairly in view of their remarkable attainments as astronomers, mathematicians or cartographers, the Jesuits were dismissed as failing in the acquisition of precise empirical knowledge. Opinion and assertion, heavily biased towards religious dogma, were said to take the place of observation and exact recording. Voyages of discovery were now expected to be team efforts by specialists who would measure, tabulate and collect specimens relevant to their particular branch of science. Cook's Pacific voyages were the model. Macartney was accompanied by a expert in chemistry and a 'machinist' in charge of scientific instruments. Two other members of the party were said to be 'conversant in astronomy, medicine and every other branch dependent upon the mathematics'. The naturalist intended for the voyage went to Africa instead, but two 'botanic gardeners' embarked. Gathering evidence about the physical sciences was, however, only a part of the embassy's functions. The Chinese themselves were the prime object of study. Exact information about them was to be used not in the service of conversion strategies but to advance knowledge in what was coming to be called the 'science of man'. Barrow wrote that the purpose of his book was 'to enable the reader to settle in his own mind, *the point of rank which China may be considered to hold in the scale of civilized nations.*'[1] He thus declared himself to be a practitioner of the very fashionable study which came to be called 'conjectural history'. Conjectural historians were concerned with collecting data about the present state of all the peoples of the earth. On the basis of this data societies were allocated places on what were taken to be universally applicable ladders of backwardness or achievement. Conjectural historians liked to suppose that they were replacing the vacuous assertions and speculations of the old travel writers with objective comparison based on firm data. Material on China had already been incorporated into the studies of man in the widest sense undertaken by Adam Smith, David Hume or Adam Ferguson. As a result of the Macartney mission, it was confidently anticipated that a great deal more would become available.

The mind of Lord Macartney was much less closed and dogmatic than that of John Barrow. Judging by an excruciating piece of verse, apparently written in 1786, older expectations lingered in his mind.

> Whether I visit China's happy coast
> Climb her fam'd wall, arts yet unrivalled boast
> With wonder gaze on her shores and floods
> Her cities, plains, her mountains rocks and woods.

[1] Ibid., p. 4.

Pass the north bounds and Tartar wilds explore
By ventrous Britons never trod before.[1]

Such effusions apart, all the members of the embassy seem to have approached China with assumptions that were generally similar. These assumptions were markedly different from those of earlier generations. The men of the 1790s were confidently sceptical. It was most unlikely that there was anything exceptional about China. It must be carefully observed and recorded. Assessments could then be made by objective standards of measurement. Western Europe and Britain provided the standard. The members of the mission were not disposed to find their own society wanting. China's examination was therefore likely to be very rigorous indeed.

If the Macartney mission approached China with intellectual preconceptions very different from those of the Sinophiles of the earlier eighteenth century, what gave them the opportunity of putting their preconceptions to the test was a spectacular growth of Britain's commercial interests in China.

In the seventeenth and eighteenth centuries the ports of southern China were transacting a huge volume of trade throughout Southeast Asia and with the Philippines and Japan. For Europeans who wished to participate in inter-Asian trade, access to certain Chinese commodities, especially silk for the Japanese market, was of great importance. This brought Dutch ships to China in considerable numbers during the seventeenth century. English involvement in Chinese trade was more spasmodic, but by the end of the century the English East India Company was developing a small direct trade between China and London. Silk was the major item exported from China at first, but it gradually came to be displaced by tea.

The saga of tea has often been told. From the first direct shipment in 1689 tea established itself as a fashionable, if costly, drink in the early decades of the eighteenth century. Over a period of some forty years, from the 1720s to the 1760s, tea consumption spread rapidly and shipments of tea into Britain by the East India Company underwent a fourfold increase. During this period the Company developed its mechanism for handling its trade in China into a form that was to last until 1833. The Company concentrated its establishments at Canton. There it was increasingly required to work through a group of 'Hong' merchants, who supplied the tea, took off British imports and accepted responsibility for ensuring that the British paid the required duties. Access to Canton was limited to the trading season and no extra-territorial rights of any kind were conceded there. Out of the

[1] Bodleian, MS Eng. Misc. d. 938, fol. 72.

trading season the factory establishment had to withdraw to Macao. The Company ships brought out British woollen cloth and metals to sell at Canton, but with the cost price of the tea shipped out exceeding the value of the British imports by about 200 per cent in the 1760s, the balance had to be made up by consignments of silver. The volume of British tea exports remained on something of a plateau from the 1760s to the mid 1780s. As was notorious, however, the volume of British tea consumption continued to increase, huge purchases by European companies being smuggled into Britain. Very high duties on legal imports gave the foreign companies and the smugglers the chance. The result was that foreign shipments of tea from Canton in the 1770s could be almost double those of the British Company, although Britain was the ultimate destination for nearly all the tea. The Commutation Act of 1784 was the remedy for this situation. Duties were cut drastically and the Company massively increased its purchases in order to undercut its foreign competitors. This strategy was successful. In the early 1780s the British Company had exported some 7 million lbs of tea compared to European purchases of some 14 million lbs. By the early 1790s the Company was buying 14.5 million lbs to 4.5 million lbs by Europeans. British tea consumption continued to grow spectacularly, fed almost exclusively by ever increasing shipments purchased by the East India Company at Canton.

In the new conditions created by the Commutation Act the East India Company and by extension the British state had a huge stake in trade with China. Tea was challenging Indian textiles as the biggest item in the Company's trade and by all calculations it was easily the most profitable. Duties on tea, even at their reduced level, which was increased again from the 1790s, were a major part of the British public revenue. This great national asset depended on access to China through the single port of Canton under the conditions of strict regulation and control which had been imposed since the mid-eighteenth century. The Chinese authorities showed no inclination to relax this system or to grant increased access. To many British people such a situation appeared to be highly unsatisfactory, even if it worked tolerably well in practice. The merchants of Canton showed themselves to be well able to expand tea supplies to Britain on a very large scale without any great rise in price. Greatly increased tea shipments required a corresponding increase in the funds available to the Company at Canton. Ideally, this would mean much larger British exports. China was an intractable market for exports from Europe, but the quantities of British woollens sold at Canton rose markedly during the 1790s. British exports in fact covered a higher proportion of the much increased tea purchases in the 1790s than they had done in the 1760s.

Left to themselves, the East India Company's Directors, while complaining bitterly in a report 1791 about the 'present cramped and humiliated state of the European trade in China' and berating the Chinese government as 'the most corrupt in the universe', had no inclination at all to do anything to change the situation. They saw no alternative to cultivating 'the present good disposition of the Chinese towards us'.[1] Any initiative on the British side would be fruitless and would only antagonise the Chinese. The Directors of the East India Company were not, however, the only British party with an interest in China by the late eighteenth century.

In the later seventeenth century the English Company, unlike the Dutch, had largely withdrawn from the inter-Asian or what British people called the 'country' trade. This was left to private British merchants, most of them in fact the servants of the Company pursuing their personal interests, who operated their own ships based on Indian ports. In the early eighteenth century English country ships, mostly owned at Madras, shipped gold from Canton to India. In the 1760s the lead in private trade to China passed to Calcutta as a consequence of the great upheavals that followed the battle of Plassey. One of the results of Plassey was that private Englishmen were able to exercise an unofficial monopoly over the disposal of a commodity that was to cast a very long shadow indeed over Anglo-Chinese relations, the opium of Bihar. In 1773 the unofficial monopoly over opium became a Company one. British control over opium production, whether private or public, meant that large quantities of opium were available in Calcutta. This was exported by private shipping to Southeast Asia or to China. An estimate for the quantity of opium landed in Macao in 1767 put it at 100 to 175 chests in a normal year, but added that 1000 chests had been imported that year with the laconic comment that extra payments had to be made to 'the Chinese' for 'conniving at its being landed, as it is a prohibited article'.[2] Direct exports of opium from Bengal to China had grown considerably by the 1790s, although the great boom was not to take place until the early nineteenth century. Country ships also carried much opium and other Bengal goods to Sumatra, where tin was bought for Canton. The greatly increased volume of 'country' trade between Bengal and China was of course a consequence of the effective control which the British could now exert over Bengal's resources, but it was also a response to the need of

[1] *House of Commons Sessional Papers of the Eighteenth Century*, ed S. Lambert, xci (Baltimore, 1975), pp. 51–60
[2] *Oriental Repertory*, ed., A. Dalrymple (London, 1793–7), i. 289.

the East India Company for funds at Canton with which to purchase tea. A famous triangular trade grew up: men who made fortunes in Bengal advanced money to country traders, who bought opium for China or goods for Southeast Asia; the proceeds of what they realised in Canton were handed over to the Company in return for bills of exchange on London. Thus private fortunes found their way from Bengal to Britain via China. The sale of Indian commodities provided the Company with about 30 per cent of the funds it needed for its tea in the 1790s. For all its future notoriety, opium was at the time of the Macartney embassy much less important at Canton than cotton from western India shipped out of Bombay. This trade grew very rapidly indeed in the 1780s. As a result, Bombay ships were by far the largest number of the British country ships going to Canton; 37 country ships were recorded for 1789.[1]

The interests of country traders and of the Company were closely intertwined. The Bombay and the Calcutta merchants needed the lure of bills on London to raise finance for their voyages and the Company needed the funds made available at Canton by such voyages. But country trade also constituted something of a challenge to the Company's extremely cautious approach to dealing with authority in China. Private merchants with an interest in China were later to become a formidable pressure group in Britain and individuals were already making representations to the government, but in the 1790s it was their activities in Canton that posed a threat to the stability of the Company's system. They had little respect for Chinese regulations. They had long flouted prohibitions on opium imports. They appointed their own agents in Canton, who tried to disregard the ban on permanent residence there. In dealing with the recognised Hong merchants they took to advancing them money awaiting remittance to Britain at high rates of interest. When some of the Hongs proved to be insolvent and unable to repay what they allegedly owed, private merchants resorted to very rough tactics indeed. In 1779 and 1780 they induced an officer commanding the squadron of the Royal Navy in India to detach a warship to Canton, in violation of many Chinese prohibitions, with importunate letters on behalf of the creditors of the Hong merchants. In 1784 these creditors were still claiming over £2 million as due to them.[2] Country traders also increasingly operated outside the Hong system altogether, dealing directly with other Chinese merchants, not officially licensed to transact business with foreigners. The greater the number of British ships coming to Canton the greater the likelihood of conflict between the crews and

[1] *Chronicles of the East India Company*, ii. 173.
[2] G. Smith's memo, India Office Records, R 10/1, pp. 145 ff.

Chinese authority. Law-abiding Indian lascars in fact constituted the majority of the crew of country ships, but what was held to be the most flagrant outrage of Chinese justice before the Macartney mission involved the execution of the European gunner of a country ship for accidentally killing two Chinese in firing a salute.

Vital as was a secure tea trade, both to the Company and the British exchequer, the dynamism of country trade to China and its potential for expansion could hardly be disregarded by any British minister with a serious interest in Asian trade, whatever the Directors of the Company might think of it. Private shipping could link China not just with India but with the Indonesian Archipelago and with the wider world of the Pacific, now definitively charted by Cook. In the 1780s, for instance, a series of projects was launched for catching sea otters on the coast of what is now British Columbia and bringing the pelts across the Ocean for sale in China. Other projects were being devised for increasing the export of British manufactured goods to Asia, including China. Balancing larger tea purchases by increased British exports was of course a very old objective of the Company's, but in the 1780s British manufacturers were beginning to press for direct access to Asian markets on private ships that, it was alleged, would convey their goods much more cheaply than the Company could. Lord Macartney personally encouraged manufacturers to look to China for an outlet for British skill and ingenuity and the Board of Trade pressed the Company to allow samples of goods to be shipped out with the embassy. The Company viewed such proposals with some misgivings. Direct shipments by private merchants were out of the question, but it was prepared to dispatch an expensive assortment of British manufactured goods on its own account

The minister who had to balance the Company's concern for a stable system at Canton with hopes for commercial expansion, no doubt largely through private trade, was Henry Dundas. Dundas was second only in standing to the prime minister himself in Pitt's ministry and was unchallenged within the government in his authority over Britain's interests in Asia. He was very receptive to ambitious schemes for expanding British trade throughout Asia and the Pacific and in principle was not over concerned to preserve the exclusive privileges of the Company. But his approach to China was cautious. He seems fully to have accepted the Company's assessment that British trade with China rested on an extremely precarious basis, which the Chinese could easily be provoked into destroying. He was unwilling to give the private creditors of the Hongs any effective support in recovering their loans or to contemplate any direct shipments to China for private exports of British manufactured goods. For the time being, the Company's monopoly of the China trade must be pre-served. But unlike the Directors, Dundas was unwilling to acquiesce indefinitely in the very restricted trading privileges allowed at Canton. He hoped that with the consent of the Chinese government Britain's commer-cial access to China could be put onto a new basis and extra-territorial rights could be gained which would give British trade effective security. If that happened, then private interests could be given their head to a much greater degree. But Chinese consent had to be obtained first; hence the strategy of sending royal envoys direct to the imperial capital at Peking. The Company was in general sceptical about such projects, believing that any mission would do more harm than good with the Chinese and that, if it was successful, their privileges would be at risk. Dundas persisted. The policy behind the embassy was his and he imposed it on the East India Company.

Charles Cathcart was appointed as the first ambassador in 1787. He died before reaching China and after an interval Macartney was persuaded to take his place in 1791 and to set out for China the following year. Macartney's embassy was a much more grandiose affair than Cathcart's would have been, but its aims as revealed in the official instructions were essentially similar. The overriding aim was to gain greatly improved com-mercial access to China for Britain. For this the main objective was a 'depot' or 'place of security', in a better location than Canton for receiving tea and distributing British manufactured goods to the biggest Chinese markets. Within this depot the British crown was to exercise full authority over British subjects. The remedying of grievances at Canton was a sub-sidiary objective to be pursued. It was hoped that the embassy would be the beginning of regular diplomatic contacts with British envoys in Peking and Chinese envoys in London. The cultural and scientific aims of the embassy were clearly spelled out in Macartney's instructions: 'A free communication with a people, perhaps the most singular upon the globe, among whom civilization has existed and the arts have been cultivated through a long se-ries of ages with fewer interruptions than elsewhere is well worthy also of this nation.' The embassy would take with it 'models of the latest inven-tions of this country', which 'cannot fail to gratify a curious and ingenious people', and it was to bring back 'specimens of their most useful produc-tions.'[1]

None of the practical objectives of the mission had been fulfilled when Macartney left China in 1794. The embassy was permitted to go to Peking

[1] *Chronicles of the East India Company*, ii. 232–41.

and then to travel on to Jehol, where it was granted an audience with the emperor. But the Chinese treated Macartney and his colleagues as emissaries bearing tribute: attempts to negotiate were deftly side-stepped and when a list of requests was presented, it was rejected. The wonders of British technology attracted little obvious interest. On the other hand, the embassy had indeed been able to study at close quarters 'a people, perhaps the most singular upon the globe' and the record of what they observed is, as I have suggested, of very great interest.

As I have also tried to suggest, the mission approached the subject of their observations, like all travellers, with certain preconceptions and expectations. Macartney in particular prided himself on having read everything in every language open to him and having talked to everybody available in Britain who might inform him about China. For him and his colleagues certain propositions were axiomatic. The accumulated recording of the Company's and private merchants' experience in Canton left no possible doubt that Chinese government at local level was rapacious and corrupt to the highest degree, while there was very little to admire about Chinese life as displayed in the great sea port. But the Jesuits had written from the vantage point of the heart of the empire at Peking. Might not things be different there? The embassy's instructions accepted that 'national character' could not be fairly judged on the basis of life in a port and even added that 'the present strength, policy and government of that empire, [are] now less understood in Europe than they were in the preceding century.'[1] Virtually for the first time, the British could observe the imperial system at the centre for themselves.

The imperial capital might indeed prove to be different from Canton, but Macartney and his colleagues approached it with what I have called 'confident scepticism'. By the mid-eighteenth century older conceptions of Chinese government as a benign patriarchal system regulated by law were coming to be discredited. Montesquieu dismissed China as 'a despotic state, whose principle is fear'.[2] Macartney's verdict after the embassy was much the same. With a bleakness that he rarely allowed to show in his journal ultimately intended for public consumption, Macartney wrote in a notebook: 'We must consider them as barbarians notwithstanding what we supposed them to be from the accounts we had of them, and therefore as Louis 14 said there is no point of honour with the Turks. They are a people not to

[1] Ibid., ii. 240.
[2] Cited in P. J. Marshall, G. Williams, *The Great Map of Mankind* (London, 1981), p. 141.

be treated with as civilized European nations …'.[1] He described the imperial government as 'the tyranny of a handful of Tartars over more than three hundred millions of Chinese'. Judicial corruption was not confined to Canton; it was general. 'As in China the interests of the emperor are always the first consideration, no property can be secured against his claims.'[2] Like all despotisms, the government was inherently unstable. In the case of imperial China, hatred of the Tartar elite, Macartney believed, made widespread insurrection almost inevitable. In elegantly turned phrases Macartney drew his famous analogy between 'the empire of China' and 'an old, crazy, first rate man-of-war, which a fortunate succession of able and vigilant officers has contrived to keep afloat for these one hundred and fifty years past, and to overawe their neighbours merely by her bulk and appearance, but whenever an insufficient man happens to have command upon the deck, adieu to the discipline and safety of the ship.'[3] When Barrow's book came out, he 'lamented that a system of government, so plausible in theory, should be liable to so many abuses in practice; and that this fatherly care and affection in the governors, and filial duty and reverence in the governed, would, with much more propriety, be expressed by the terms of tyranny, oppression and injustice in the one, and by fear, deceit, and disobedience in the other.'[4] For him 'China was worn out with old age and disease'.[5]

The embassy's instructions assumed that enlightenment might still be found lurking in Peking and that the regime would respond in their sense rationally to an appeal to join in mutually beneficial diplomatic, commercial and cultural exchanges. Macartney freely admitted that he had entertained such hopes. These hopes had been dashed and Macartney confessed to a severe disappointment 'in the immediate failure of success in a favourite undertaking, be the remote consequence ever so flattering'.[6] Nevertheless, he hoped that imperial authority might be invoked to remedy some of the grievances of the Company at Canton and that further embassies on a less grand scale would probably be received. He was by no means prepared to admit total failure in the diplomatic objectives of the mission, while the embassy had enjoyed unprecedented opportunities to observe China and the Chinese.

---

[1] Bodleian, MS Eng. Misc., f. 533, fol. 7.
[2] *Journal*, pp. 236, 241, 242.
[3] Ibid., p. 212.
[4] *Travels*, p. 360.
[5] Ibid., p. 222.
[6] *Journal*, p. 152.

The intellectuals on the mission would have betrayed all their cultural convictions if they had not sought to formulate sweeping generalisations about the Chinese society which they had observed. They had no such inhibitions: China was duly categorised and ranked. There was no doubt that China was a 'civilised' and by another standard a 'commercial' society. But it suffered from a fundamental defect that distinguished it from Europe: it was a totally stagnant civilisation in which the processes of change and development had atrophied long ago. At the time of Marco Polo, Macartney wrote, by comparison with Europe, the Chinese were 'a very civilized people ..., but not having improved and advanced forward, or having rather gone back, at least for these one hundred and fifty year past, since the conquest by the northern or Manchu Tartars; whilst we have been every day rising in arts and the sciences, they are actually become a semi-barbarous people in comparison with the present nations of Europe.'[1] According to Staunton, the Chinese have not 'advanced in manners, and in arts and knowledge of every kind'.[2] Barrow thought that the institutions of China had not changed for some two thousand years.[3]

Explanations of China's failure to change were readily to hand. The Chinese government had a great deal to answer for. That despotic regimes destroyed individual initiative, the mainspring of human inventiveness and therefore of change, was conventional wisdom virtually beyond question. Barrow was the most dogmatic exponent of the idea that a repressive government had crushed all individuality out of the Chinese. They had been cowed due to 'the habits in which they have been trained, and to the heavy hand of power perpetually hanging over them'.[4] The system allowed no men of hereditary rank or independent fortune to emerge and so there were no intermediate orders pursuing their own ends independent of the government. The power wielded by fathers over families enforced repression throughout society: 'a tyrant ... to command and a slave to obey, are found in every family'.[5]

Joseph Banks, the great promoter of every scientific inquiry, was very much involved in the planning of the Macartney embassy. He recognised that China now possessed only 'the ruins of a state of civilisation', but he still believed that 'the useful as well as the ornamental branches of science are

[1] Ibid., p. 384.
[2] *An Authentic Account of an Embassy from the King of Great Britain to the Emperor of China*, 2 vols. Dublin, 1798, ii. 330.
[3] *Travels*, p. 394.
[4] Ibid., p. 176.
[5] Ibid., p. 151.

likely to derive infinite advantage' from the mission. He pressed Macartney to take properly qualified technicians with him. 'It is highly probable', he wrote, 'that a few practical men admitted among them would in a few weeks acquire a mass of information for which if placed in the industrious and active hands of English manufacturers the whole revenue of the Chinese empire would not be thought sufficient equivalent'.[1] The members of the embassy found little to sustain his expectations. In a stagnant society achievement in the arts and sciences was not to be expected. Dr Gillan reported ignorance in every branch of the sciences, as he understood them. 'In all the mechanical arts and manufactures', he concluded, 'the Chinese content themselves with the processes and methods of operation already known, which they imitate without the smallest change or deviation, without ever inquiring whether they might be improved by any addition or alteration in the mode of conducting them.'[2] Macartney thought that the Chinese 'in every respect to science ... are certainly far behind the European world'. He was very struck by the lack of knowledge or curiosity displayed at the imperial court, by comparison with what the Jesuits had written of K'ang-hsi as a patron of learning.[3] Barrow was characteristically caustic. 'In their present state, they are totally incapable of appreciating any thing great or excellent in the arts and sciences ... At this moment, compared with Europe, they can only be said to be great in trifles, whilst they are really trifling in every thing that is great.'[4]

Even Banks' 'ornamental branches of science' failed to evoke much enthusiasm in the embassy. Macartney brought back paper hangings in considerable quantity for his friends, and had an appreciative eye for the splendours of the summer palace outside Peking or of Jehol. But he thought that 'the defect of the Chinese in all these things is the pushing them to extravagance which is generally the natural death of taste, occasioned by a plenty of riches which grows hypocandrical and capricious'.[5] Barrow characteristically found very little to impress him. Japanese porcelain was better than Chinese but neither would 'bear a comparison' with the work of 'the ingenious Mr Wedgwood'. 'The whole of [Chinese] architecture, indeed, is as unsightly as unsolid; without elegance or convenience of design, and without any settled proportion.' He uttered the despairing cry of the western

[1] Material kindly communicated by Dr John Gascoigne.
[2] *Journal*, pp. 279–303.
[3] Ibid., pp. 264–6.
[4] *Travels*, pp. 343, 355.
[5] Bodleian, MS Eng. Misc. f. 534, fol. 11.

tourist throughout the ages: 'There is not a water-closet, nor a decent place of retirement in all China'.[1]

Barrow and Macartney differed somewhat in their analysis of China's agrarian economy. Both accepted that the population was enormous and that much of it lived in dire poverty, but Barrow doubted whether there was as yet very acute pressure on land. The poverty of the mass of the population and the incidence of famine arose rather from small scale farming using inefficient techniques.[2] Macartney disagreed. He believed that Chinese farming methods were well suited to the conditions which he encountered. 'The Chinese are certainly the best husbandmen in the world'. There were, however, too many people for the land to support. Thus there was not 'always sufficient employment for the people, whose multitude is so great as to exceed the means of subsistence by labour'. On either interpretation, 'a large proportion of the population' in Macartney's words, lived in 'misery'[3] Even Barrow, however, conceded that Chinese people were extremely industrious. Macartney believed that: 'It is certain that wherever the Chinese go, their activity and industry contribute much to the melioration of the place and make commerce flourish.'[4]

At his bleakest in his writings about the Chinese at the time of the first opium war, Palmerston could note in a letter to Sir Henry Pottinger that Chinese negotiators still clung to 'that tone of affected superiority with which it has invariably been the systematic policy of the Chinese to cloak in their intercourse with foreigners the real weakness of the empire; you are so well acquainted with the Asiatic character and so much accustomed to deal with orientals that it is unnecessary for me to instruct you to stop at the outset any attempt of this kind.'[5] This is not quite the language of Dundas, Macartney or Staunton, even if it is very close to that of Barrow, but the sentiments are not very far from theirs. There were no real mysteries left about China after the embassy. The Chinese were becoming just another 'Asiatic' or 'oriental' people, whose dispositions could already be well understood by a man like Pottinger with long Indian service. The weakness of China was too evident for claims to superiority not to be dismissed as 'affected' even in 1793. British commentators in the age of the opium wars were to depict China in very much the same terms as those used by the

---

[1] *Travels*, pp. 305, 330, 333.
[2] Ibid., pp. 566, 575–86.
[3] *Journal*, pp. 188, 244.
[4] Bodleian, MS Eng. Misc. f. 533, fol. 15.
[5] H. B. Morse, *International Relations of the Chinese Empire*, 3 vols. (London, 1910–18), i. 659.

Macartney embassy. The gap between China and Europe was now enormously wide. China was a weak and vulnerable giant, stranded in the past. Its rulers were incapable of reform or of adjusting to the modern world. Their rule prevented any significant development of Chinese society. Technology was backward and the mass of the people were sunk in poverty. The hardworking and long suffering populace of China deserved a better fate.

As far as British interests were concerned, the regime remained as intractable in 1839 as it had been in 1793. Nothing much had improved. The programme of concessions worked out for the Macartney mission was as relevant as ever: Britain still wanted access to more ports, 'a depot' or 'place of safety' in which trade could develop without oppressive restrictions, better conditions at Canton and regular diplomatic contact. Reasoned persuasion seemed to stand no more chance of success than had proved to be the case in 1793. Hopes for a more accommodating attitude after the embassy had proved groundless. Was there not now a case for using force to compel the old order to change its ways and thus both to remove impediments to British interests and to start processes of change which could not but improve the lives of ordinary Chinese?

The crisis over opium in 1839 provided at least the pretext for using force and compelling the Chinese to grant the concessions so long desired. The men of 1793 were aware of force as a theoretical option but there was no breakdown of relations at Canton and even if there had been, it is scarcely conceivable that Pitt and Dundas would have been willing to put the Company's trade at risk for highly speculative benefits from the use of force. In 1833 the Company had lost its monopoly and its capacity to impose restraint disappeared. Palmerston put the recovery of debts due from the Hong to private merchants high on the list of grievances to which the Chinese must give satisfaction.

Yet the triumph of private trade is surely not the whole story. Although the men of 1793 shared most of the assumptions of Palmerston, total conviction of the superiority both of the British character over that of the Chinese and of the British capacity for waging war, and were coming to accept that the Chinese imperial regime was wholly unregenerate, they still had genuine inhibitions about the use of force, which later generations did not share. Palmerston believed that the time for negotiations without the spur of force had passed for ever and he summarily dismissed Charles Elliot for failing to apply enough force. Macartney rejected the use of force on the grounds of 'reason' and 'humanity'. In doing so he was expressing ideals wholly characteristic of his time. The ethos of the late eighteenth-century voyage of discovery included a total commitment to peaceful contact with indigenous peoples. This was movingly expressed in the President of the Royal Society's 'hints' to Cook and Banks for the first voyage. 'To have it still in view that shedding the blood of these people is a crime of the highest nature:- They are human creatures, the work of the same omnipotent author, equally under his care with the most polished European; perhaps being less offensive more entitled.'[1] This ethos was very evident in the instructions for the embassy. 'We have no views but the general interest of humanity', Macartney was told or told himself. Since such sentiments might not sound absolutely convincing to Chinese statesmen who were well aware of what was happening in India, Macartney should assure them that Britain had always acted on the defensive in India.[2]

The contradiction between ideals and how the British actually conducted themselves throughout the world was of course glaring. The late eighteenth-century British state was highly militarised and its rulers took immense pride in its warlike prowess. Even the humane Cook believed that Pacific islanders needed to be made aware of the firepower of British ships as well as of the purity of British intentions. Macartney travelled in a warship with a small detachment of soldiers from whom, it was hoped, the Chinese might derive 'no useless idea of our military character and discipline'.[3] Macartney at first sight seems an unlikely candidate to be a sentimental pacifist. He was a man of government, relentless in his pursuit of office and honours. Long administrative experience seems to have inclined him to a pessimistic authoritarianism. Neither the Irish (a people among whom he evidently had ceased to count himself) nor the French could be governed by anything other than 'severity'. Reform of British government must be attempted 'gradually, all sudden changes threaten danger'. He was extremely sceptical about the anti-slavery movement.

Nevertheless, too much cynicism, either about eighteenth-century ideals for the peaceful diffusion of knowledge and trade throughout the world or about an idealist streak beneath the insufferable self-regard and the wary caution of Macartney, would probably be undue. Macartney envisaged himself as 'seeing the world in all its quarters, "mores hominum et urbes", enlarging the mind, expanding the views, in benefiting the state, giving honourable example and gratifying noble ambition'. Yet he could also write

[1] *Journals of Captain James Cook, i. The Voyage of the Endeavour 1768–71*, ed., J. C. Beaglehole (Cambridge, 1955), p. 514.
[2] *Chronicles*, ii. 234, 237–8.
[3] Ibid., ii. 236.

mockingly of the career of arms, which was assumed to constitute 'a young man's felicity and the most respectable situation in life for a mature aged man', but was in reality no more than a man's 'being sold for life ... to draw his sword, right or wrong, and murder men, women and children, at home or abroad, without knowing why or wherefore.'[1] Late eighteenth-century mental barriers to endorsing the use of force on the Chinese may have been little more than paper thin. Nevertheless, there was still a mental barrier to be broken before we are in the age of the opium wars, even if we are in that age in nearly all other respects. Whatever else we may think about him, Lord Macartney is not yet Lord Palmerston.

---

[1] These expressions of his opinions at the time of the embassy are drawn from Macartney's notebooks, Bodleian, MS Eng. Misc. f. 533, f. 534.

Historical Anachronism: The Qing Court's Perception of and Reaction to the Macartney Embassy

Zhang Shunhong

LORD MACARTNEY'S EMBASSY TO CHINA was an important event in the history of relations between Britain and China. It was a mission from the most powerful country in the world to the most powerful one in the East. In a sense it was also a challenge from a newly rising industrial power to a relatively stagnant feudal state. The embassy's experience in China and its transactions with the Qing court have been well researched.[1] This paper thus only focuses on a rethinking of the Qing court's perception of and reaction to the embassy. It will try to reveal to what extent the court failed to understand the embassy and the international background against which the mission was initiated, and how the court's perceptions influenced its decisions.

The Qing court's perception of the Macartney embassy underwent several stages. At the beginning, both the Qianlong emperor and the mandarins considered the embassy to be a tribute mission, coming to present congratulations for the emperor's birthday, with no other motive. As early as 22 October 1792, Guo Shixun, Governor of Guangdong province and acting Viceroy or Governor General of Guangdong and Guangxi provinces, and Shengzhu, Superintendent of the Canton Customs, jointly sent a memorial to Qianlong reporting that the King of England was now sending an envoy

---

[1] For details of the Macartney embassy's experiences in China see E. H. Pritchard, *The Crucial Years of Early Anglo-Chinese Relations, 1750–1800* (Washington, 1936); J. L. Cranmer-Byng, 'Lord Macartney's Embassy to Peking in 1793, from Official Chinese Documents', *Journal of Oriental Studies* 4:1–2 (1957–58), pp. 117–87; Alain Peyrefitte, *L'empire immobile, ou le choc des mondes* (Paris, 1988), translated as *The Collision of Two Civilisations: The British Expedition to China in 1792–4* (London, 1993). The latest work in English on the subject is Aubrey Singer's *The Lion and the Dragon: The Story of the First British Embassy to the Court of the Emperor Qianlong in Peking 1792–1794* (London, 1992). Recent works in Chinese include three articles in Zhu Jieqing, ed., *Zhongwai Guanxi Shi Lunwenji* [Symposium on the history of Sino-Foreign relations] (Henan, 1984) and also Zhu Yong, *Buyuan dakai de Zhongguo damen* [China's closed door: the diplomacy of the eighteenth century and China's destiny] (Nanchang, 1989).

to China to present congratulations for the emperor's birthday; in their view this showed that the British people were reverential and friendly.[1] The emperor was apparently pleased to hear this news. On 3 December 1792 he issued an edict to the Viceroys and Governors of the coastal provinces ordering them to make careful preparations for the reception of the British envoy and to help conduct him and his tribute articles to Beijing as soon as he landed on the coast; there was to be no delay or disorder.[2] Qianlong then issued detailed instructions to the Grand Councillors and some Viceroys and Governors regarding the way in which Macartney should be treated. For instance, his edict of 22 February 1793 directed that, when the British tribute envoy reached the coast, well disciplined officers and soldiers ought to be sent there and banners and weapons should be polished up in order to show seriousness and solemnity. This was not because such foreigners might have suspicious intentions, but because of the customary regulations concerning the treatment of foreign missions. Discipline and order, solemnity and vigour, were to be displayed to give the foreigners feelings both of awe and veneration.[3] On 24 July 1793 the emperor issued another edict to Liang Kentang, Viceroy of Zhili province, and Zhengrui, Salt Administrator of Changlu in Zhili province, who had been instructed to welcome Macartney at the coast near Tianjin. This edict ordered that the British tribute envoy should be treated moderately and the mandarins should be neither servile, nor overbearing towards him. However, in the eyes of the emperor, Macartney, as the first envoy from Britain, should be treated differently from those sent by such countries as Burma and Vietnam, which paid tribute frequently.[4]

In the Qing court's reactions to the Macartney embassy, the emperor himself played a crucial role. In his view it was 'a good thing' that Britain sent an envoy to present tributes and congratulations for his birthday. He thus entertained a lenient attitude towards the conduct of the British at the early stage of the mission. This can be clearly seen from the following events. In late May 1793 the Commissioners of the East India Company decided to send a small vessel, the *Endeavour*, under Captain Proctor to sail up the

---

[1] *Zhupi zouzhe waijiaolei* [Memorials to the Emperors — Diplomacy] (hereafter *ZZW*), vol. 24, no. 1. (China number one archives).

[2] *Qing Shilu* [Veritable records of the reigns of the Qing dynasty] (hereafter *QSL*) (Beijing, 1986), vol. 26, pp. 1029–1030; *Zhanggu Congbian* [Collected historical documents] (hereafter ZGCB), 'Documents on the Macartney Embassy', pp. 5–6.

[3] *QSL*, vol. 27, p. 12.

[4] Ibid., p. 131.

eastern coast of China to contact the embassy.[1] After Proctor reached Zhejiang province, Chang Lin, its Governor, sent a memorial to the emperor, saying that Ma Yu, Garrison Commander of Dinghai, should be severely punished for letting Proctor sail away without awaiting a reply from the Governor himself and that he had asked the Governors of some coastal provinces to watch Proctor's navigation.[2] But the emperor instructed that as Proctor came to look for the tribute envoy without any other intention, Chang Lin should tell him personally that it was up to him whether he stayed or went. The Governor was instead criticised for his excessive reaction. Other coastal Governors also received the imperial instruction that Proctor should be permitted to stop or go according to his own decision.[3] As to the ceremonial, the emperor issued an edict on 3 August which said that if Macartney and his suite refused to *koutou* when they met Viceroy Liang or other mandarins, they should not be urged to do so, rather they were to be allowed to behave according to the ritual custom in their own country.[4] On the same day, Zhengrui sent a memorial to the emperor reporting that the British Chief and Assistant Envoys considered themselves to be of high rank and insisted on meeting others on an equal footing. For this reason, Zhengrui himself did not go personally to visit them, and instead he ordered two other conducting mandarins of lower rank, Qiao Renjie and Wang Wenxiong, to go to see Macartney and Staunton on their boat in order to get information on the King's letter and the tribute articles.[5] After receiving this report, the emperor criticised Zhengrui on 5 August for regarding himself as important and superior, and said that even if the envoys did perform the *koutou* to Zhengrui, he would not be honoured by it himself, and if they did not do so no damage was done. As they had sailed for nearly one year, particular consideration should be shown them. Pedantic haggling over ceremonial issues was not the proper way of treating people from afar.[6]

Such a favourable attitude towards the embassy, however, did not last long. When Qianlong saw the list of tribute articles he was angered by the 'arrogant' explanations of the instruments, and his opinion of the embassy changed. On 6 August, only one day after he criticised Zhengrui for his

[1] The court was not aware that Captain Proctor was actually sent by the commissioners of the East India Company, and believed that he was despatched by the King of England to see whether Macartney had safely arrived in China.

[2] J. L. Cranmer-Byng, 'Lord Macartney's Embassy to Peking in 1793', pp. 129–130.

[3] *ZGCB*, 'Documents on the Macartney Embassy', p. 8.

[4] *QSL*, vol. 27, p. 136.

[5] *ZZW*, vol. 25, no. 6.

[6] *QSL*, vol. 27, p. 138.

strict attitude towards Macartney on the ceremonial issue, Qianlong announced that the list of tribute articles bore many exaggerations. The British did not know what greatness was and thus considered themselves possessed of unique and secret skills and boasted of the excellence and rareness of their own manufactures. In the list it was also written that a 'Commissioner' was being sent to China. This further infuriated Qianlong who wrote that as Britain was sending a mission to pay tribute, there was no reason to call the envoy 'Commissioner'. He then ordered that both Macartney and Staunton were to be called 'Tribute Envoys'.[1]

The period from 6 August until Macartney's arrival at Rehe (Jehol) was a crucial stage in the court's perception of the embassy. During this time Qianlong attempted to assess both the nature of Macartney's real conduct and the value and merits of the tribute articles. Macartney had been reported to be reverential and obedient. Now Qianlong was suspicious of this and ordered Zhengrui to make careful observations of Macartney's deportment to see whether he betrayed any sign of haughtiness. Zhengrui's memorial of 17 August reported to the emperor that Macartney was indeed modest, reverential and obedient.[2] Though temporarily satisfied with Macartney's conduct, Qianlong still had many queries about the tribute articles. It was said in the memorials from Zhengrui and Liang Kentang that some instruments were very big and delicate, especially the planetarium which needed one month to be set up and could not be moved and dismantled afterwards. This to a certain extent shook the emperor's confidence in the superiority of China's technology and science. He was slightly satisfied when he received the memorial sent on 18 August by Jin Jian, President of the Board of Works, and Yi Ling'a, Vice-President of the Board, who had been appointed to take charge of the tribute articles in the capital. In the memorial Macartney was reported to be impressed by the magnificence of the buildings of the imperial palaces and to have said that all the eight articles left in the capital could be displayed in one building, the Zhengdaguangming Palace [the Great Hall] in the Yuanming Yuan.

Meanwhile, Qianlong was trying to assess the nature of the planetarium and other instruments. On the one hand, he ordered some Chinese craftsmen, eunuchs and Jesuit missionaries at the court to watch the British craftsmen putting together the tribute articles. At the same time he instructed Zhengrui, Jin Jian and Yi Ling'a to send quick and detailed memorials on this issue. But he did not get much information from them

[1] Ibid, pp. 139–40.
[2] *ZZW*, vol. 25, no. 16.

for a number of days. On 29, 30 and 31 August he lost his temper and furiously blamed these three officials for still keeping silent on questions as to the exact size of the scientific instruments, how the British craftsmen were setting them up, whether the Chinese craftsmen, eunuchs and missionaries already understood how to operate and dismantle the planetarium and other instruments after they had watched their installation by the British, and whether one month was really needed to put together the planetarium. Qianlong also ordered Jin Jian and some other mandarins to compare the celestial and terrestrial globes brought by Macartney with the ones exhibited in the imperial palaces.[1] On 30 August Jin Jian and Yi Ling'a sent a memorial to the emperor in which they wrote that all eight articles including the planetarium had been set up within six days, that the craftsmen, eunuchs and missionaries had already understood how to operate, dismantle and set up these instruments, and that the celestial and terrestrial globes and the lustres were similar to those in the imperial palaces. The other articles were also reported to be by no means unique: one of them was said to be not so well made as similar items already in the imperial palace. In this memorial the scientific instruments of the embassy were simply underestimated.[2] This memorial was in a sense significant in the emperor's assessment of the science and technology embodied in the embassy's presents. It had the effect of restoring and strengthening the court's confidence in China's superiority and contributed to its failure to recognise the real importance of the embassy's scientific instruments. With a strong confidence in China's superiority in science and technology, the emperor assumed that once Macartney saw that China had similar and better instruments and had also skilled craftsmen who were versed in astronomy, geography and clock repairing and who understood how to operate, dismantle and set up the tribute instruments, he would not be so 'arrogant'. The emperor did not make further inquiries about the planetarium and other instruments. Evidently he had already come to the conclusion that Macartney exaggerated the importance of the tribute articles. After the mission arrived at Rehe Qianlong showed little curiosity in the scientific instruments which were in his view not very useful; China, he felt, did not need such 'curios'.

At this crucial stage the emperor made a serious mistake. Although he was once very eager to get information on the tribute articles he never told the mandarins to inquire how such instruments were produced. Rather, he fre-

[1] *QSL*, vol. 27, pp. 159–62; *ZGCB*, 'Documents on the Macartney Embassy', pp. 48–51.
[2] China Number One Archives, ed., *Yuanming Yuan* (Shanghai, 1991), volume one, pp. 351–54. This work is a compilation of Qing documents related to the Yuanming Yuan and contains a number of memorials on the Macartney embassy (pp. 330–60).

quently suggested in his edicts that Macartney exaggerated their value and merits. Influenced by this attitude the conducting mandarins restrained themselves from inquiring into the manufacture of these scientific instruments. For instance, in their memorial of 9 August to the emperor, Liang Kentang and Zhengrui said that the envoy's account of his tribute articles was exaggerated 'so when we met him, we did not ask how the articles were produced'.[1] The emperor did order skilled Chinese personnel to watch the British craftsmen setting up the instruments, but the purpose was only to learn how to operate, dismantle, and repair such instruments so that they would not become more useless after the British went home. What was more vital, namely the technology of producing such scientific instruments, was ignored by the court. Macartney was right in observing that the emperor and his courtiers were not interested in science and showed little curiosity for the instruments brought by the embassy. This lack of interest in science and curiosity for the embassy's presents led to the failure of the Qing court to realise Britain's advanced technological and scientific achievements and China's backwardness in this respect.

On the other hand, Qianlong was now more concerned with ceremonial. On 14 August an imperial order was issued to Liang Kentang and Zhengrui, instructing them to persuade Macartney to perform the *koutou* when he had an audience with the emperor at Rehe. Zhengrui's report convinced Qianlong that Macartney would do so, for he was learning how to perform it. This, of course, was not the truth. After his arrival at Rehe Macartney still declined to perform the ceremony. The emperor was again infuriated and said on 9 September that he was very displeased by the envoy's 'unfamiliarity' with the ceremonial. He attributed Macartney's conduct to his lavish treatment at the hands of the mandarins on the way to Rehe, totally unaware that Macartney's refusal to perform the *koutou* was actually the challenge of an ambassador from a powerful colonial state, with ideas of Western diplomacy, to the established diplomatic or tributary system of China.[2] It had nothing to do with the mandarin's treatment of the envoy. Qianlong, however, reacted to the embassy very much as he perceived it. He ordered the local mandarins to treat the mission with less generosity. In his view it was not worthwhile treating such 'ignorant' people with much courtesy or favour. This was the first time the emperor considered Macartney 'ignorant'.

[1] *ZZW*, vol. 25, no. 13.
[2] *QSL*, vol. 27, pp. 170–171.

It should be pointed out that on 11 September Qianlong issued a different edict which said that the Chief and Assistant Envoys were quite reverential and obedient when they met the Grand Councillors that day. As they now showed loyalty and obeyed the Celestial regulations they should still be treated with favour and courtesy. The 14th of September was the day when the emperor granted his first audience to the embassy. Qianlong appeared to be satisfied with Macartney's performance as suggested by the poem he wrote that day. The first two sentences of this poem stated that 'Formerly Portugal paid tribute: now Britain is paying homage'.[1]

The emperor's complacency, however, disappeared after he read the translation of George III's letter which Macartney presented to him at this audience and which requested that a British envoy should be allowed to reside permanently in Beijing. Such a request was unacceptable to the court which was deeply disturbed by this unprecedented suggestion. On 15 September Macartney asked for permission for Captain Mackintosh to leave Rehe early for Zhushan, where the *Hindostan* was anchored. Three days later Macartney handed another note to Heshen, the Grand Secretary, in which he again asked that Mackintosh might be allowed to go without delay to Zhushan in order to resume the care of his ship there, and that the staff on the ship might be permitted to purchase a cargo of tea. He also recommended sending a European missionary with Mackintosh who would then conduct to Beijing the two mathematicians, Robert Hanna and Louis-François Lamiot, who had intended to enter into the Emperor's service and who were now on board the *Hindostan*. Furthermore, Macartney repeated his desire to have free communication of correspondence with Canton.[2] Although these points were not totally rejected, the court appeared to have felt pestered by Macartney's seemingly endless requests. On 23 September the emperor issued an edict to Chang Lin, now the Viceroy of Guangdong and Guangxi provinces, and the Governors of Guangdong and Zhejiang provinces, saying that as the British envoy came from afar, and was fairly

[1] J. L. Cranmer-Byng, 'Lord Macartney's Embassy to Peking in 1793', p. 172. Liu Jiaju has recently argued that there was some kind of 'secret diplomacy' between Macartney and the Qing court before the audience and that Macartney did perform the *koutou* to the emperor. Qianlong's satisfaction with Macartney's performance at the audience appears to support his argument, but the prevailing view is that Macartney never *koutou*ed; Liu Jiaju, 'Ying shi Majiaerni jinjian Qianlong huangdi de liyi wenti' [Conflict over ceremony on the Occasion of the English Ambassador Macartney'] A Paper presented to a conference on the early modern history of China, Taibei, China, 1988.
[2] *ZGCB*, 'Documents on the Macartney Embassy', pp. 59–62; J. L. Cranmer-Byng, ed., *An Embassy to China: Being the journal kept by Lord Macartney during his Embassy to the emperor Ch'ien-Lung 1793–1794* (London, 1962), p. 141.

reverential and obedient, he was treated with great consideration and courtesy. However, after his arrival at Rehe he made many impertinent requests and was frequently haughty. Such a foreigner was indeed 'ignorant'. The request that a British envoy should be allowed to reside in Beijing was rejected. The king of that country might seek pretexts to make trouble. As the country was very remote and they had to travel for a very long time to get here, they probably did not dare to launch a war against China. But since they were ignorant and presumptuous, they might cause disturbances on the coast, especially at Macao. It was thus necessary to make preparations in advance.[1] This should be done unobtrusively so as not to arouse suspicions among the foreigners and the local people. Similar imperial instructions were issued on 1 October 1793 to Chang Lin, Guo Shixun, and the Governors of the provinces of Jiangsu, Anhui and Jiangxi.[2]

After his return to Beijing Macartney presented on 3 October six requests to Heshen concerning British trade with China, as he had been instructed to before he left Britain.[3] These requests further irritated and worried the court which refused to consider almost all of them. Two days later the emperor again instructed the Viceroys and Governors of the coastal provinces to make preparations for the disturbances the British might cause. Now the court was anxious to send Macartney away.

In response to Macartney's conduct and requests the Qing court did decide to take certain actions. The emperor ordered that all the posts, garrisons and beacons near the routes along which the embassy would travel should be put into good order in advance, and troops were to be well disciplined so as to make an imposing impression on the British. When the envoy and his suite passed through prosperous parts of the country, they should be allowed to make observations so that they would realise that China was prosperous and rich, and her people were enjoying peace and happiness. This, it was felt, would curb the haughtiness of these foreigners. The authorities at Canton were instructed by the court to prevent collaboration between the British and the Portuguese in any actions against China. They were also urged to take measures to prevent the 'stubborn and intractable' British merchants from monopolising the trade at Canton. Local officials were warned not to extract additional or illicit duties from British commercial ships to avoid giving any pretext to the British for making trouble.

[1] *QSL*, vol. 27, pp. 182–83; *ZGCB*, 'Documents on the Macartney Embassy', pp. 64–65.
[2] *ZGCB*, 'Documents on the Macartney Embassy', pp. 69–71.
[3] Cranmer-Byng, *Embassy to China*, p. 150; see also H. B. Morse, *The Chronicles of the East India Company Trading to China, 1635–1834* (Oxford, 1926), vol. 2, pp. 214–15.

According to the imperial instructions coastal defence was to be strengthened, the navy was to be on the alert to prevent the British occupying islands secretly, and British merchant ships visiting any ports other than Canton were to be expelled immediately. Finally, local authorities in the coastal provinces were instructed to inhibit any collusion between 'treacherous' local inhabitants and the foreigners.

Macartney left Beijing on 7 October. On his way to Canton, he had more talks with Song Yun, a Grand Councillor, who conducted him to Hangzhou and Chang Lin, who escorted him from Hangzhou to Canton. In their memorials to the emperor, Macartney was often reported to be obedient and grateful to the emperor. This lessened Qianlong's anger with the British envoy and he was later even inclined to receive future envoys from Britain. By the time Macartney left China the court had become much less anxious to strengthen the country's coastal defences and ready their troops. Thus the court's actual responses to the embassy were very limited.

What the Qing court did attempt to do was no more than a reinforcement of the established closed-door policy which was becoming increasingly unsuitable to the changing international environment. But in the view of the court such measures would be sufficient to cope with possible external threats. In the face of the challenges embodied by the Macartney embassy what the court needed to do was to take an open-door policy towards the outside world, and to learn from the West as it did in the late nineteenth century. It also needed to reform feudal institutions and start to move towards a modern society. The Qing court under Qianlong failed to do this and its reactions to the Macartney embassy can be said to have been anachronistic. This was not in the sense that it refused Macartney's requests, but that it did not respond in a way that would enable China to deal with the new problems imposed by a changing world. The court's anachronistic reactions were closely correlated with its incorrect perceptions of the mission and its international background. Macartney was considered as a tribute envoy from a small state in the West, not as an ambassador from a powerful colonial country. Only after Macartney arrived at Rehe, did the court realise that the 'Tribute Envoy' came to China not only to present congratulations for the emperor's birthday, but also with other aims. The court was never fully aware that the objects of the mission were mainly commercial and diplomatic. To a certain extent it did anticipate the seriousness of a possible confrontation with Britain after refusing Macartney's requests; however, in its view Britain was only a relatively strong state in the West and while the British, being ignorant and unaware of China's greatness, might take rash action they would only cause minor disturbances in the coastal areas. The most worrying thing for Qianlong was rather the possibility of collusion between local inhabitants and trouble-making foreigners.

The Qing court indeed failed to perceive the real challenges embodied by the Macartney embassy. The presents brought by the mission were the products of Britain's advanced science and technology and were no doubt challenging to China's sense of superiority.[1] Unaware of their importance, the court did not realise the extent of China's backwardness. Macartney's refusal to perform the *koutou* was also a defiance of China's established diplomatic or tributary system. But the court attributed it to his ignorance and haughtiness. The requests put forward by Macartney regarding British trade with China again challenged China's foreign and trading policies. Britain was then undergoing a rapid process of industrialisation and was becoming the world's factory, thus needing more markets for its manufactures. Though the Qing court had a vague idea of Western colonization, it was unconscious of the fact that Britain was the country with the largest overseas empire, one which was rapidly expanding in Asia. In a word, the court was ignorant of international affairs. The Macartney embassy rightly observed that the Qing court knew little about the outside world, and still held the illusion that China was the centre. Ironically, of course, the court also held Macartney to be 'ignorant'.

At the time of the embassy China was comparatively well known to Britain. In the eighteenth century British society witnessed a Chinese vogue which reached its peak in the middle of the century and writers in Britain frequently referred to things Chinese. Many publications related to China were printed. What were known as 'arguments from the Chinese' were even used by the opposition in British politics against the government.[2] However, Britain was little known to China although the two countries had had commercial relations for a long time. In the whole of the eighteenth century not a single work dealing particularly with Britain was published in China. The British were often confused with other Europeans. It would be wrong, however, to say that Chinese writers had no ideas about Britain. An authentic work entitled *Qingchao wenxian tongkao* [A textual compilation

---

[1] For details on the scientific instruments Macartney brought to China see J. L. Cranmer-Byng and Trevor H. Levere, 'A Case Study in Cultural Collision: Scientific Apparatus in the Macartney Embassy to China, 1793', *Annals of Science* 38 (1981), pp. 503–25.
[2] T. C. Fan, 'Chinese Fables and Anti-Walpole Journalism', *Review of English Studies* 25 (1949), p. 141.

of the literature of the Qing dynasty], compiled under an edict of the emperor Qianlong and completed around 1786, did have a short entry for Britain (or, rather, England). There were two crucial points there. Firstly, that Britain had a colony (though one only was implied) and secondly that some British products, such as clocks, were 'incomparably ingenious'.[1] The first point would lead one to think of Britain as a colonial power and the second indicated that Britain possessed advanced technologies in certain respects. This was important for the Qing court to reach a sound assessment of British science and technology, but neither the emperor nor his courtiers seemed to have paid much attention to such a record. What Macartney said about the delicate nature of the scientific instruments he brought, as discussed earlier, was simply considered by the court as exaggeration. The Qing court's ignorance of Britain was indeed in sharp contrast to British knowledge of China. At the time of the embassy the court was still wondering where exactly Britain was whereas at the same time there were Britons who were attempting to put China into a proper place in the scale of world civilizations. John Barrow, for example, Comptroller of the Macartney embassy, attempted to do this in his *Travels in China* [1804].

In the contact of these two countries at this time China was indeed the one observed while Britain was the observer. Members of the Macartney embassy published a number of works about China whilst the Qing court produced none on Britain. The ambassador himself made many observations which were even closer to the realities of Chinese life than the Qing court's own notions of China. For instance, Macartney took the view that China was becoming 'semi-barbaric' compared with Europe, which was making great progress in science and technology. It is true that in the eighteenth century China was lagging behind Europe, especially in the field of science and technology, but the Qing court still assumed that China was the most advanced country in the world. The court also held the illusion of China's military superiority over other countries. As China's military force was stronger than that of her neighbours it was consequently assumed that she was also stronger than the Western nations. Macartney, however, noted that the Chinese military force was very weak. They were:

> totally ignorant of our discipline, cumbersomely clothed, armed only with matchlocks, bows and arrows, and heavy swords, awkward in the management of them, of an unwarlike character and disposition ...

[1] *Qingchao Wenxian Tongkao*, vol. 298.

[and so] they would make but a feeble resistance to a well-conducted attack.[1]

Macartney's opinion was again closer to the truth as evidenced by later events. The embassy was indeed a challenge to China. In this sense it also provided an opportunity for the Qing court to realise the extent of China's backwardness and to understand the real and changing international situation. But the court failed to do so, and it felt no necessity to reform China's established institutions, and to change the closed-door policy to suit the development trend of the whole world. Threats were greatly underestimated. It can be argued here that without a correct perception of the outside world, the court would be unlikely to respond in the right way to external challenges.

Why the Qing court failed to properly perceive the Macartney embassy and its international background is a complicated question. Here are only some brief ideas. China had long been more advanced than its neighbours and the Qing rulers had thus been imbued with the mentality of sino-centrism. They were neither interested in understanding the outside world, nor willing to communicate with it. Since the early eighteenth century the court had been, on the whole, practising a growing closed-door policy. Foreign trade on the coast was confined to Canton from the middle of the century. There was little intellectual communication with the West. The separation from the rapidly developing part of the world and the long-term ignorance of external affairs helped to hinder the court from correctly perceiving the Macartney embassy and its international background. China during Qianlong's reign experienced economic prosperity and social stability, and the court won a number of wars, most recently defeating the Gurkhas. This certainly strengthened the sense of superiority in China's military force and civilization among the Qing rulers. All of these factors contributed to the failure of the court to understand the Macartney embassy and the global situation. Such failure largely explained why the court failed to react in the right way to the challenges embodied in the Macartney embassy. Qianlong's refusal to reform the established systems and take an open-door policy made China more backward compared to Britain and Europe as a whole. Time was lost in catching up and keeping pace with the West, especially in terms of science, technology and military force. In consequence China had to endure the disasters of the nineteenth century.

[1] Cranmer-Byng, *Embassy to China*, p. 203.

THE MACARTNEY MISSION: A BICENTENNIAL REVIEW

TSENG-TSAI WANG

1

BY REASON OF HER RELATIVE ISOLATION from other major centres of civilization, such as those in Mesopotamia and the Mediterranean regions, and by virtue of the fact that there was no other power to compete with her in both size and cultural accomplishments in the Eastern Asian World, China tended to regard herself as 'central' in a cultural as well as a geographical sense. Convinced of their cultural superiority, the Chinese treated all peoples who had not been nurtured in their traditions as inferior beings and beyond the pale of civilization. In this they were not unlike the rulers of Imperial Rome when they surveyed the barbarian tribes beyond the Rhine and the Danube. The very term *i* or 'barbarian' as applied to foreigners meant simply 'not yet Sinicized' and it can be traced back to very ancient times.[1] Imperial China was a universal dynastic empire rather than a nation-state,[2] and her sole mission was always to educate, to conquer and to invest legal rights in her part of the world. *The Books of Odes* expressed this theory in the following utterance: 'Under the wide heaven, there is no land that is not the emperor's, and within the seaboundaries of the land, there is none who is not the subject of the emperor.'[3] The emperor was so revered that any mortal must perform the ceremony of the *k'ou-t'ou* (three kneelings and nine knockings of the head on ground) in his presence. This was the ceremony which was demanded by the Chinese Court of foreign envoys when they were granted audience until as late as 1873.[4]

---

[1] Mary Wright, *The Last Stand of Chinese Conservatism* (Stanford, 1957) p. 222; Wu Hung-chu, 'China's Attitude towards Foreign Nations and Nationals Historically Considered', *The Chinese Social and Political Science Review* 10.1 (Jan., 1926), p. 15.
[2] John K. Fairbank, 'Synarchy under the Treaties', in J. K. Fairbank (ed.), *Chinese Thought and Institutions* (Chicago, 1957), p. 208.
[3] *Book of Odes, Hsiao-ya: pei-shan*, chapter II, translated by Immanuel Hsü in his *China's Entrance into the Family of Nations* (Harvard, 1960), p. 6. Cf. J. Legge, *The Chinese Classics*, IV part II, p. 360.
[4] For details, see W. W. Rockhill, *Diplomatic Audiences at the Court of China* (London, 1905).

The non-recognition of equal states found its counterpart in the governmental organization of Imperial China. The imperial government of the Ch'ing period handed down since the Ch'in and Han dynasties (221 BC–AD 220) was a patriarchal absolutism headed by the Son of Heaven. There was no foreign office in its various branches of government, and this was because what China knew were only affairs of dependencies and tributaries, for which the existence of a foreign office was unnecessary. Thus the Chinese non-recognition of equal states was coupled with the absence of a foreign office. So, too, from the standpoint of international law and diplomacy the ground occupied by pre-modern China was totally unintelligible. Diplomacy as the application of intelligence and tact to the conduct of official relations between the governments of independent states did not exist in the Chinese world order. China's foreign relations in ante-treaty days were usually conducted under the so-called 'tributary system'.[1]

China's foreign trade, which served for so long as a means to keep her tributaries under control, was conducted in accordance with her own traditional tributary system even after western contacts were made. The European mercantile invasion of China's coast coincided with the collapse of the Ming and the rise of the Ch'ing dynasty. In 1684, after the political situation in China was stabilized, the K'ang-hsi emperor issued an edict opening the coast ports to foreign trade but this permission only lasted until 1757. After this date, due to the problem of control and administration, the Ch'ien-lung emperor practically prohibited foreign trade at any port other than Canton.[2] The Canton system, which had become crystallized and legally confirmed by 1760, was imposed to the disadvantage of foreign traders. The foreign merchants were restricted by numerous regulations, which became more elaborate as time went on and which aimed at segregating or quarantining them in their factories, thereby causing them

[1] For details of this system, see John K. Fairbank and S. Y. Teng, 'On the Ch'ing Tributary System', *Harvard Journal of Asiatic Studies*, 6.2 (June, 1941), pp. 135–246, (This article can also be found in the same authors' *Ch'ing Administration: Three Studies*, Harvard, 1960); J. K. Fairbank, 'Tributary Trade and China's Relations with the West', *The Far Eastern Quarterly*, 2.2 (Feb., 1942), pp. 129–49; *Trade and Diplomacy on the China Coast* (Harvard, 1953), I, chapter II; M. Frederick Nelson, *Korea and the Old Orders in Eastern Asia* (Baton Rouge, La., 1945), part I, 'The International Society of Confucian Monarchies'. For a collection of recent brilliant discussions of the Chinese world order and the tributary system, see J. K. Fairbank, ed., *The Chinese World Order* (Harvard, 1968).

[2] Different dates have been given by different Western accounts (the space does not allow the author to enumerate them all). The dates given here are based on Chinese information. See *Shih-erh-ch'ao tung-hua lu* (The Tung-hua records of the twelve reigns) *K'ang-hsi period*, 8, p. 24; *Ch'ien-lung period*, 16, pp. 48–49.

much inconvenience. This policy reflected China's suspicion of foreigners and foreign countries. It was strengthened by the fact that the agrarian economy of China was largely self-sufficient. Whatever trade with foreigners was permitted was conceded to show the emperor's gracious treatment of men from afar, but it could be dispensed with at any time. The Chinese, interested in preserving their territory from military, political and cultural encroachments, would tolerate foreign trade under strict supervision, but nothing more. Owing to the fact that the early trade was largely one-sided, the Chinese came to believe that the peoples of Europe were dependent on China for their well-being and that China did not need the West as the West needed China. They considered their strongest weapon to be the threat to cut off all trade, a weapon which always seemed effective because the foreigners were always willing to yield on matters in dispute in order to continue the profitable trade. To worsen matters further, the formal policy of China was hostile to commerce until recent times, and the mercantile calling was not regarded as honourable. For this reason, it has been a misfortune to Great Britain and the West generally that they were brought into contact with China through commerce.

It was under the conditions stated above that the British came into contact with China. They soon found that they were sailing in a strange sea.

2

Despite the fact that British efforts to establish intercourse with China began long before the East India Company was chartered on the last day of 1600, the British were late-comers on the Far Eastern scene in comparison with the Portuguese, the Spanish and the Dutch. In fact, it was not until 1637 that a flotilla of four ships under John Weddell opened up communication directly with China, and not until the year 1699 that the real foundation of the permanent trade at Canton was established by the voyage of the *Macclesfield*. From then on, however, British trade grew so rapidly that before the middle of the eighteenth century the British had outstripped all their competitors and their trade was greater than that of all other foreign countries combined.[1] By the middle of the 19th century the China trade

[1] For a detailed survey of the early Sino-British relations and international rivalries of the old Canton trade, see H. B. Morse, *The Chronicles of the East India Company Trading to China*, 5 vols. (Oxford, 1926–9); Peter Auber, *China* (London, 1834); J. B. Eames, *The English in China* (London, 1909); A. J. Sargent, *Anglo-Chinese Commerce and Diplomacy* (Oxford, 1907); E. H. Pritchard, 'Anglo-Chinese Relations during the Seventeenth and Eighteenth Centuries', University of Illinois *Studies in the Social Sciences*, 17.1–2, pp. 1–244 (Urbana, Illinois, 1929); 'The Struggle for Control of the Chinese Trade during the Eighteenth Century' *The Pacific Historical Review*, 3.3 (Sept.,

was so important to Britain that Sir J. R. G. Graham declared in the House of Commons on April 7, 1840, when the House met to debate the China war, that one-sixth of the whole united revenue of Britain and India depended on it.[1]

British ascendancy in the Canton trade was reflected in the supreme position enjoyed by the Select Committee representing the East India Company at Canton. This managed the Company's affairs in China and carried out the orders of its Court of Directors in London. Throughout the years until the Company's monopoly of the China trade was abolished in 1834, the Chinese tended to regard the President of the Select Committee, the *taipan* as they used to call him, as the spokesman for the entire body of foreign merchants and to hold him responsible for the conduct of foreign trade. One of the interesting cases illustrating this fact occurred when Russia was prohibited from taking part in the Canton trade, in 1805. An edict to this effect was forwarded through the Hong merchants to the Select Committee with a direction to them to deliver this edict to the Russians.[2]

Influenced by the industrial revolution which took place first in Great Britain in the second half of the eighteenth century, the British came to be more and more concerned with finding new markets for their products. In view of the preponderance and importance of British commercial interests in China, the British government naturally wanted to establish normal diplomatic relations with China and to improve the conditions of the trade by putting it on a treaty basis. China on the other hand, interested in maintaining her old system and wishing to limit her contact with the West to the commercial level as well as to confine foreign influences to the factories, was quite unprepared for any new departure. The British government, however, decided to break down the barriers by sending an embassy directly to the court in Peking.

1934), pp. 280–95; Sir William Forster, *England's Quest of Eastern Trade* (London, 1933); Edwin O. Reischauer and J. K. Fairbank, *East Asia: The Modern Transformation* (Vol. II of *A History of East Asian Civilization*) (London, 1965), pp. 15–75; Hsia Hsieh, *Chung-Hsi chih-shi* (A record of Sino-Western events; 1868); Chang I-tung, 'Chung-Ying liang-kuo tsui-tsao-ti-chieh-ch'u' (The earliest Sino-British contacts'), *Lishi yanjiu* or *Li-shih yen-chiu* (Historical Studies), 5 (1958), pp. 27–46.

[1] *Hansard: Parliamentary Debates*, 3rd series, Vol. LIII. p. 670.

[2] *Foreign Records of East India Company* (MSS in the Indian Office, No. 11, under Memoir: Intercourse with China, pp. 277–79), quoted in Eames, *English in China*, p. 134.

So, in the autumn of 1791, the British government, after the abortive embassy of 1787–8 under Charles Cathcart, MP, decided to send Lord Macartney to China.

George, Earl of Macartney, was a distinguished diplomat and colonial administrator. Prior to his appointment as ambassador extraordinary and plenipotentiary to China, he had served in many public offices. He had been envoy-extraordinary to St Petersburg, a member of the Irish and British Parliaments, Chief Secretary for Ireland, and Governor of Grenada. In 1766, he was created Lord Macartney, Baron of Lissanoure in the Irish peerage. He was appointed Governor and President of Fort St George (Madras) in December, 1780. He returned to England in January, 1786, and was offered the Governor-Generalship of Bengal, a post he refused: it fell, ultimately, to Lord Cornwallis. He was promoted to Viscount Macartney of Dervock in 1792 after his appointment as ambassador to China and was further advanced to the title of Earl of Macartney in the County of Antrim in 1794, all of these within the Irish peerage.[1]

On May 2, 1792, Lord Macartney attended the Court of St James in order to have the honour of being presented to kiss His Majesty's Hand, and on the following day he was officially appointed 'Embassador Extraordinary and Minister Plenipotentiary from the king of Great Britain to the Emperor of China'. On the same day he was sworn a Privy Councillor, and Staunton got his official appointment as 'Secretary to the Embassy and Minister Plenipotentiary in the absence of the Embassador' as well.[2] In order to avoid any appearance of being a mere commercial emissary, the ambassador was to carry a letter from George III to the Emperor of China, and the commercial nature of the undertaking was to be disguised under the ostensible object of conveying the King's congratulations and good wishes to the emperor upon the attainment of his eighty-third birthday. The entire cost of the embassy — salaries, maintenance, and all charges — was to be met by the East India Company. The excellent assortment of presents — with a total value of £15,610 — included those taken over from the Cathcart embassy, which had cost £2,486. These presents were packed in 600 packages and were later carried into Peking by 90 wagons, 40 barrows, 200 horses, and 3,000 coolies. This was also paid for by the Company. To convey the ambassador, the Admiralty dispatched the 64 gun HMS *Lion*, commanded by Captain Sir Erasmus Gower; to carry his suite and the pre-

---

[1] For details, see John Barrow, *Some Account of the Public Life of the Earl Macartney* (London, 1807). Vol. I; Helen H. Robbins, *Our First Ambassador to China* (London, 1908); *Dictionary of National Biography*, Vol. XXXIV (London, 1893), pp. 404–406.
[2] Barrow, *Life of the Earl of Macartney*, p. 347.

sents, she was accompanied by the Company's ship *Hindostan* and the tender *Jackal(l)*.[1]

The instructions given to Lord Macartney, were dated September 8, 1792.[2] They first outlined the importance of British trade in China and pointed out that the conditions under which it had operated had been most discouraging. In order to avoid unnecessary complications at Canton, the ambassador was recommended to proceed directly to Tientsin unless otherwise advised by dispatches from the commissioners at Canton. As for ceremonies to be observed in audience with the Chinese emperor, the ambassador was ordered to conform to all ceremonials which might not impair the honour of the British sovereign or lessen his own dignity, but he was also advised not to let trifling punctilio stand in the way of the important benefits which might be obtained by engaging the favourable disposition of the emperor and his ministers. He was instructed to state to the Chinese court that the British concerns were purely commercial and he was to be prepared to lull any Chinese suspicion caused by the British position in India. The ambassador was also empowered to negotiate a treaty of friendship and alliance with China. His instructions emphasized the importance and desirability of establishing normal diplomatic relations with China by exchanging envoys and the plan to leave Staunton as a resident minister at Peking in the event of the ambassador's death or absence. In the ambassador's credentials and again in the King's letter to the emperor[3] it was reiterated that Britain hoped to maintain a permanent resident minister in Peking (Staunton being accredited for this service) and that there were abuses in the trade which the King would like to have remedied. Furthermore, in order to avoid possible Dutch hostility to the embassy, Lord Auckland, the British ambassador to Holland, was instructed to seek Dutch cooperation, which was given.[4]

Under these circumstances then, the whole embassy, consisting of 95 persons, or some 800 people if soldiers, botanists, artists, and servants were included, set sail from Spithead on September 26, 1792.[5] The Ch'ien-lung

---

[1] Morse, *Chronicles*, II, p. 216.

[2] The full text of it can be found in ibid., pp. 232–42.

[3] Ibid., II, pp. 244–47.

[4] E. H. Pritchard, 'The Crucial Years ...', pp. 302–303.

[5] *Lord Macartney's Journal*, Sept. 26, 1792. There are three editions of this Journal available in print. They are contained respectively in Barrow, *Life of the Earl of Macartney*, II, pp. 163–517; Robbins, *First Ambassador to China*, pp. 180–440; J. L. Cranmer-Byng, *An Embassy to China* (London, 1962), pp. 61–303. The earliest edition of it, that given by John Barrow, is unreliable, since a comparison of this with Robbins' and Cranmer-Byng's accounts indicates that Barrow has altered the language on occa-

emperor learnt of the coming of the Macartney mission on December 2, 1792,[1] and his reaction to it was warm enough. He expressed great satisfaction when he was informed of it and he ordered through a court letter that the embassy should be permitted to travel to Tientsin and thence to Peking. He ordered, too, that the governor-generals and governors of the provinces on the coast should lavish every possible attention on the embassy.[2] The emperor was very pleased that so many rescripts and edicts were issued in succession to make preparations for the reception of the embassy. One thing must be made clear here, namely that the emperor showed condescension and kindness to Lord Macartney not because he was the representative of the sovereign of an important power but because he was a newcomer arriving to witness the glories of the Celestial Empire after a full year's sea voyage, and was thus in a different category from those who brought tribute regularly from nearby Annam, Burma, and other places.[3] As a matter of fact, the ambassador was always referred to as 'tributary envoy from Britain' and was repeatedly put on the same level with the Mongol Princes, and the envoys from Burma and Annam; the emperor planned to fete all of them together at Jehol.[4]

On the other hand, Lord Macartney had very high hopes and great ambitions when he sailed from Portsmouth. In March, 1793, he arrived at Batavia, where dispatches from the Company's commissioners at Canton, stating that the announcement of the embassy had been favourably received by the emperor and that preparations were being made for his reception, had arrived.[5]

Lord Macartney and his suite landed at Taku, at the mouth of the Peiho, on August 5, 1793. He was met by Liang K'ên-t'ang, governor-general of Chihli at the *Hai-shen miao* or the Temple of the Sea God. After the usual compliments, the governor-general talked much of the emperor's satisfac-

---

sions to suit his purpose. Cranmer-Byng's account is even fuller and more satisfactory than Robbins'. He also has done a good job identifying people and places mentioned in the text. Robbins has given a wrong date of departure for the embassy, 1793 instead of 1792. See Robbins, *First Ambassador*, 180; Cranmer-Byng. *Embassy to China*, p. 61; see also Barrow, *Life of the Earl of Macartney*, II, p. 163; Sir George L. Staunton, *An Authentic Account of an Embassy from the King of Great Britain to the Emperor of China*, (London, 1797), II, p. 53.

[1] *Chang-ku ts'ung-pien* (Collected historical documents; Peking 1928–9) (Cited below as *CKTP*), I, pp. 1–2.

[2] Ibid., I, p. 5.

[3] *CKTP*, II, p. 12; *Ch'ing shih-lu* (Veritable records of successive reigns of the Ch'ing dynasty) (*CSL*), *Ch'ien-lung period*, 1431: pp. 15–16.

[4] *CKTP*, II, pp. 9, 12; V, pp. 16, 29; *CSL*, *Ch'ien-lung period*, 1428: pp. 9–11.

[5] Staunton, *Authentic Account*, I, pp. 235–41.

tion at the arrival of the embassy, and of his wish to see the ambassador in his summer palace at Jehol where the court always resided at that season. Lord Macartney expressed his willingness to go to Jehol to pay his respects to the emperor, but said that some of the presents might be damaged during so long a journey so it would be advisable to leave the more delicate ones at Peking. He was particularly struck with the governor-general's ease, politeness, dignity and kindness.[1] The embassy arrived at Tientsin on August 11, 1793. There they were met by the Governor-general and the legate, Chêng-jui. The latter's unfriendly disposition was only too obvious. Soon Lord Macartney quarrelled with him over the problem of the presents because the legate insisted that all of them should be brought to Jehol, and it was not until the governor-general had intervened that he changed his demand. It was also decided to proceed to Tungchow by boat and afterwards by land to Jehol. The embassy moved on up the Peiho with flags on the boats conveying it inscribed with characters 'The English Ambassador bringing tribute to the Emperor of China' [*Ying-chi-li kung-shih*]. This was known to the ambassador; but considering it not a matter of primary importance and fearing that if he was unsuccessful in redressing the matter, he might jeopardise the success of his mission, or even abruptly terminate it, he made no protest and decided to shut his eyes to the flags, preferring to let his ignorance be assumed.[2]

Owing to the attempted intervention by the East India Company in the war between the Chinese and the Gurkhas of Nepal in Tibet, the Chinese seem to have become inclined to suspect some sinister intention concealed beneath the offers of gifts and friendship on the part of Britain. But Lord Macartney had no news of the affair in Tibet beyond some information he got from conversations with Chinese officials on August 16, on his arrival at Tungchow on the way to Peking.[3] However, the main difficulty arose from a matter of ceremony.

The emperor showed deep concern over the matter of the *k'ou-t'ou* ceremony from the time when Lord Macartney reached China. Doubting whether the ambassador had *k'ou-t'ou*ed as required, or had merely taken off his hat and bowed as he did when the imperial edict concerning the em-

---

[1] *Lord Macartney's Journal*, in Robbins, *First Ambassador to China*, pp. 254–58; Cranmer-Byng, *Embassy to China*, pp. 73–74; *CKTP*, III, pp. 18–20.
[2] *Lord Macartney's Journal*, in Robbins, *First Ambassador to China*, pp. 260–69; Cranmer-Byng, *Embassy to China*, p. 88; Staunton, *Authentic Account*, II, pp. 130–31; *An Historical Account*, p. 306. Staunton said the insignia carried by the flags was, 'Embassador Bearing Tribute From The Country of England.'
[3] *Lord Macartney's Journal*, in Robbins, *First Ambassador to China*, pp. 268–69; Staunton, *Authentic Account*, pp. 272–76; Morse, *Chronicles*, II, p. 224.

bassy was made known to him at his first meeting with the governor-general of Chihli and then at the imperial banquet held in his honour at Tientsin, the emperor issued an edict through a court letter dated August 14. This instructed the legate to inform the ambassador tactfully in the course of conversation that not only envoys of the vassal states had to perform the ceremony, but even their princes had to do the same when they were in audience with the emperor.[1] Again, instructions from the Grand Council to the legate dated August 18, stated that the ambassador must first practise the etiquette and only when he was versed in the salutation of *k'ou-t'ou* ceremony might he be ushered into an imperial audience.[2]

The *k'ou-t'ou* question was first raised by the legate and other conductors on August 15. The ambassador was informed, after some arguments, that it was a ceremony to be performed before the emperor which 'never had been, and never could be, dispensed with.' Lord Macartney, however, refused to go any further than to pay the emperor the same sort of obeisance that he would pay to his own sovereign.[3] The matter became more urgent as a result of the above-mentioned edict and instructions. It was taken up again heatedly on 19 and 25 August.[4] A deadlock was created by the legate's insistence on unconditional compliance and Lord Macartney's refusal to undergo the ceremony. In order to remove the difficulty, Lord Macartney decided to make a direct appeal to Ho-shên, the most powerful grand councillor and the emperor's favourite, who the emperor used to call first minister. He accordingly drew up a note to him dated August 28, four days before he left Peking for Jehol. He proposed in that note a solution involving reciprocal concessions: he would perform the *k'ou-t'ou* on condition that one of the ministers of the Chinese court, equal with him in rank, should perform exactly the same ceremonies of homage before a picture of His Britannic Majesty. On the following day the note was delivered to the legate who promised to transmit it to Ho-shên at Jehol. But we know that he returned the note to Macartney after it had been forwarded to Ho-shên.[5]

[1] *CKTP*, V, p. 31.

[2] Ibid., VII, p. 41.

[3] *Lord Macartney's Journal*, in Robbins, *First Ambassador to China*, pp. 266–67; Cranmer-Byng, *Embassy to China*, 84–85.

[4] *Lord Macartney's Journal*, in Robbins, *First Ambassador to China*, pp. 172, 282; Cranmer-Byng, *Embassy to China*, pp. 90, 98.

[5] *Lord Macartney's Journal*, in Robbins, *First Ambassador to China*, pp. 282–84; pp. 297–98; Cranmer-Byng, *Embassy to China*, pp. 99–100, pp. 117–18; Staunton, *An Authentic Account*, II, pp. 143–44; pp. 208–13; Sir George Thomas Staunton, *An Historical Account of the Embassy to the Emperor of China*, London, 1797, pp. 310–11.

The embassy set out from Peking on September 2 and entered Jehol in state on September 8. Meanwhile the emperor became furious at the ambassador's non-compliance.[1] Lord Macartney made it quite clear that either the ceremony should be reciprocal or he should be allowed to use the same homage as he would pay his sovereign, that is kneel on one knee and kiss the emperor's hand. The Ch'ien-lung emperor was liberal by the standards of the Chinese emperors, and he finally determined to accept the British point of view. It was decided on September 10 that the ambassador should be permitted to perform the British ceremony although the kissing of the emperor's hand was to be dispensed with.[2] As Staunton observed, 'This determination relieved the Ambassador from a load of much anxiety.'[3] The matter was formally and officially settle on September 11 when Lord Macartney had a meeting with Ho-shên and other chief ministers. On that occasion he was informed that because of the great distances which he had travelled to pay his respects to the emperor, he would be allowed to perform the English ceremony, that he would be permitted to deliver the King's letter into the emperor's hands, and that the time for the first audience was set for September 14.[4] On the same day, an imperial edict was issued saying that the British were now 'sincerely obedient and all followed the prescribed rules of the Celestial Empire', and that it would be advisable to let their errand be fulfilled by giving an audience.[5]

Accordingly, Lord Macartney was given an audience under a magnificent tent in the Wan-shu Yuan, or the palace park, on the morning of September 14, 1793. On September 17, being the emperor's birthday, the embassy went again to the imperial court to take part in the celebrations.[6] On both occasions, the ambassador and his suite were permitted to kneel

[1] *CKTP*, VII, pp. 52–54; *Lord Macartney's Journal*, in Robbins, *First Ambassador to China*, pp. 292–99.
[2] *Lord Macartney's Journal*, in Robbins, *First Ambassador to China*, pp. 298–300; Cranmer-Byng, *Embassy to China*, pp. 118–19; Staunton, *Authentic Account*, II, pp. 213–19.
[3] Ibid., II, p. 219.
[4] *Lord Macartney's Journal*, in Robbins, *First Ambassador to China*, pp. 300–302; Cranmer-Byng, *Embassy to China*, pp. 120–21; Staunton, *Authentic Account*, II, pp. 220–21.
[5] *CKTP*, VII, p. 54.
[6] *Lord Macartney's Journal*, in Robbins, *First Ambassador to China*, pp. 303–307, 313–14; Cranmer-Byng, *Embassy to China*, pp. 122–24; pp. 131–36; Staunton, *Authentic Account*, II, pp. 224–39, 256.

upon one knee and make profound bows.[1] This was really an unusual concession on the part of the emperor.

After having presented his credentials to the emperor and having attended the imperial birthday celebrations, the ambassador was still not able to open negotiations on the basis of the instructions he had received. He tried to start negotiations with Ho-shên and other chief ministers on September 11 when they first met each other. After the audience, he was conducted twice by Ho-shên and others on a tour round the palace parks on the 15th and 17th of September respectively. On each occasion, Lord Macartney repeatedly tried to turn the conversation to the subject of his mission, but the grand councillor adroitly avoided discussing his suggestions.[2] He also endeavoured without success to introduce the subject of the embassy during a conversation with the emperor when the embassy was invited to the court to attend a play.[3] The splendid embassy was viewed solely as a tributary and congratulatory mission and was treated as such. Furthermore, from the moment it landed at Taku on August 5, 1793, until its arrival by the inland route at Canton on December 19 in the same year, the embassy was entirely cut off from all communications with the outside world. All the members of it were, in fact, little more than 'prisoners in silken bonds.' After the Chinese government had decided to refuse the British demands, edicts were issued urging the authorities concerned to take precautionary measures to prevent the British from stirring up trouble.[4]

The embassy set out for Peking on September 21 and reached it on the 26th. After the imperial court returned to the capital on the 30th, Lord Macartney made strenuous efforts to start negotiations again. In an attempt to avoid the immediate dismissal of the embassy by the Chinese, he sent a note to Ho-shên on October 1 proposing to ask the emperor's leave to depart for Canton soon after the Chinese new year, which fell early in

[1] All British official narratives agree that the embassy did not perform the *k'ou-t'ou*. Most of the Chinese documents or works which mention the embassy are either silent on the subject of the ceremony performed or just make equivocal statements. Some non-British writers, however, say or imply that the embassy *k'ou-t'ou*ed. Judging from circumstances at that time, it is fair to say that the embassy did not perform the *k'ou-t'ou* ceremony. For details, see E. H. Pritchard, 'The Kowtow in the Macartney Embassy to China in 1793', *The Far Eastern Quarterly*, 2.2 (Feb., 1943), pp. 163–203; Rockhill, *Diplomatic Audiences at the Court of China*.

[2] *Lord Macartney's Journal*, in Robbins, *First Ambassador to China*, pp. 301–302 , 308–311, 315–318; Cranmer-Byng, *Embassy to China*, pp. 120–21, 124–29, 131–36.

[3] *Lord Macartney's Journal*, in Robbins, *First Ambassador to China*, pp. 318–19; Cranmer-Byng, *Embassy to China*, pp. 137–38.

[4] *CKTP*, VIII, pp. 64–65, IX, pp. 70–72; *CSL: Ch'ien-lung period*, 1435: pp. 9–11, 29–31, 32–33; 1436: pp. 1–4; Morse, *Chronicles*, II, pp. 223–25.

February, 1794. This was followed by a meeting with Ho-shên, as well as other Chinese chief ministers, at the Yuan-ming Yuan on the following day. An embarrassing situation occurred, for while the ambassador was trying to do his best of open talks on the exchange of envoys and other subjects concerning the two countries, the grand councillor suggested that the embassy should depart as soon as possible on the pretext that the winter was approaching and the climate would soon become disagreeable to the British.[1] After all his attempts to broach the subject of his mission were brushed aside Lord Macartney presented a note containing his requests to Ho-shên on October 3. These requests constituted a modest charter of rights for British trade since they were mainly concerned with commerce.[2] But the Chinese government, on the other hand, had already made their decision by September 23 and an imperial edict rejecting the British request to have a resident minister in China bears that date. Since Western diplomatic practices were entirely unknown to the Chinese at that time, they were suspicious of the request, thinking that the British intended some sinister work of espionage in China.[3] Meanwhile, they decided to dismiss the embassy as early as possible. They first fixed the date October 9 for its departure and then changed it to October 7.[4]

By this time Lord Macartney was convinced that further attempts to delay his departure would accomplish no good purpose. The situation caused by the French Revolution in Europe also served to strengthen his determination to leave. He agreed with the Chinese to leave Peking on October 7, 1793.[5] So the splendid embassy finally won no more than three imperial

[1] *Lord Macartney's Journal*, in Robbins, *First Ambassador to China*, pp. 323, 325–31, Cranmer-Byng, *Embassy to China*, pp. 142, 144–49 ; Kuo T'ing-i, *Chin-tai Chung-kuo shih* (Modern Chinese history), I, p. 237; Staunton, *Authentic Account*, II, p. 329.

[2] *Lord Macartney's Journal*, in Robbins, *First Ambassador to China*, pp. 331–33, Cranmer-Byng, *Embassy to China*, pp. 149–50; Kuo T'ing-i, *Chin-tai Chung-kuo shih*, I, p. 243.

[3] *CKTP*, VIII, pp. 64–65 ; *CSL, Ch'ien-lung period*, 1435: pp. 9–11 (with slightly differing wording from the one found in the *CKTP* collection.) This edict served as instructions to the Chinese ministers and was different in content from the emperor's letter to the King. E. H. Pritchard seems to have confused them. (See 'The Crucial Years …', p. 345).

[4] *CKTP*, VIII, pp. 63–64, 66–67; *CSL, Ch'ien-lung period*, 1435: pp. 28–29.

[5] *Lord Macartney's Journal*, in Robbins, *First Ambassador to China*, pp. 333–38, Cranmer-Byng, *Embassy to China*, pp. 151–55; Staunton, *Authentic Account*, II, pp. 334–35. As we know, the National Convention of France declared war against Britain, Holland and Spain on February 1, 1793. (See *An Encyclopedia of World History*, compiled and edited by William Langer, Revised and 3rd edition, p. 582).

edicts which plainly manifested the Ch'ien-lung emperor's attitude to Great Britain and its King. All in all, they rejected the British requests.[1]

With deep disappointment, Lord Macartney left Peking for Canton on October 7, 1793. He left Canton for home on January 10 and landed at Portsmouth on September 5, 1794. Lord Macartney had a meeting with the Prime Minister, William Pitt, at his house in Downing Street on September 22.[2]

3

Thus ended the mission of the first fully accredited ambassador from Great Britain to China. It was almost a complete failure. The basic reason for its failure was that China, not knowing her proper position in the world, was averse to foreign intercourse. Lord Macartney was, however, more fortunate than Lord Amherst whose mission, some twenty-four years later, ended without even an audience with the Chia-Ch'ing emperor.

It was the cultural differences between China and the West that were responsible for those failures; China knew nothing of modern international affairs when the East met the West. The tributary system with which China had managed her foreign relations until the mid-nineteenth century was an outgrowth of the cultural pre-eminence of China in the Eastern Asian world. It implied a traditional Chinese world order of surrounding states, which benefited from trade with China's superior civilization while acknowledging its superiority with tribute missions. In a tradition-bound society, like China's, with a civilization unique in its resistance to institutional change, it was only natural that the people should have the idea that their system was the best one and adequate to handle relations with all foreign peoples. The Chinese believed they were bound to defend the existing system to the last. We must keep this factor in mind when we try to explain why China's response to the Western challenge was so tardy and ineffectual and why she found it so difficult to adjust to the multistate system of modern international politics. In dealing with historical facts, sympathetic understanding is sometimes needed. In relinquishing her claim of supremacy over other states, a nation like traditional China was acting in a matter in which she could not but feel that her customary *raison d'être* was

[1] *CKTP*, III, pp. 18–19; *CSL, Ch'ien-lung period*, 1435: pp. 11–20; IX, pp. 73–74; Liang T'ing-nan, *Yüeh-hai kuan-chih* (Gazetteer of the maritime customs of Kwangtung), 23: pp. 8–13.
[2] *Lord Macartney's Journal*, in Robbins, *First Ambassador to China*, p. 391, Cranmer-Byng, *Embassy to China*, p. 217; Barrow, *Life of the Earl of Macartney*, I, p. 356; *The Times*, September 23, 1794, p. 2.

likely to be destroyed. After the 1858 Sino-British Treaty of Tientsin had been signed, Lord Elgin commented in his report to Lord Malmesbury that: 'The concessions obtained in it from the Chinese Government are not in themselves extravagant ... but in the eyes of the Chinese Government, they amount to a revolution, and involve the surrender of the most cherished principles of the traditional policy of the Empire. They have been extorted, therefore, from its fears.'[1]

The author tends to say, that all Western and Chinese charges against each other, if any, were unfounded in the early Sino-European contacts since what was involved was a matter of culture or way of life both in national and international spheres. It was not until after the peace of Westphalia in 1648 that there was any form of foreign office in any Western state,[2] presumably because the idea of universal empire, as of universal church, lingered on until that time. Western scholars pointed out, as we see, that Europeans usually call East Asia the 'Far East', (even the Australians who were immigrants from Europe, were doing so until recently); they did not know, consciously or unconsciously, that East Asia lies to their north and not far from them.[3] It will be difficult for us to understand such a state of affairs if not in terms of culture. The world has become a small village in our own time but in the days of Lord Macartney it was still large enough to let different countries take their different courses.

---

[1] *F. O. Print*, Vol. 764, No. 338, Elgin to Malmesbury, July 12, 1858.
[2] L. Oppenheim, *International Law*, ed., H. Lauterpacht, 7th ed. (London, 1948–52), I, p. 763.
[3] Arnold J. Toynbee, ed., *Half the World: The History and Culture of China and Japan* (London, 1973), p. 9.

THE MACARTNEY EMBASSY IN THE HISTORY OF SINO-WESTERN RELATIONS

JAMES L. HEVIA

I WANT TO BEGIN MY COMMENTS on the Macartney embassy in the history of Sino-Western relations with a quotation that should be familiar to all of you.

> The Celestial Empire, ruling all within the four seas, simply concentrates on carrying out the affairs of Government properly, and does not value rare and precious things ... we have never valued ingenious articles, nor do we have the slightest need of your Country's manufactures.[1]

These are, of course, a few phrases from what is perhaps the most often quoted passage in histories of Sino-Western relations. They come from the letter written in 1793 by the Qing emperor Qianlong to King George III and comprise part of the response to requests made by the British ambassador, Lord Macartney. Since 1922, when Bertrand Russell argued that 'no one understands China until this document has ceased to seem absurd' (1922: 47),' the content of this letter has often been used to demonstrate the profound cultural distance between Europe and China at the dawn of modernity.

The Qianlong letter was one of a number of things the embassy brought back to England. Yet another was the word *koutou*, a name for the notorious act that so outraged several generations of 19th-century European and American diplomats and, as 'kowtow' continues in common usage up to the present as a scornful term for shamefully subservient behaviour.[2]

---

[1] Among many other places, the passage appears in Parker, 1896; Teng and Fairbank, 1954: 19; Mancall, 1963: 18; Cranmer-Byng, 1963: 340; Hsü, 1970: 206; Rozman et. al. 1981: 22–23; and Spence, 1990: 122–123.

[2] Macartney himself never seems to have used the term, referring instead to 'genuflexions and prostrations' (Cranmer-Byng, 1963: 84). Rather according to the *Oxford English Dictionary* it came into usage in England through John Barrow's account of the embassy (1806: 213), where it is spelled as 'koo-too'. The more familiar form, 'kowtow' appears in accounts of the Anglo-French invasion of North China in 1860.

My concern today is with the careers of the Qianlong letter and the *koutou* in some Euro-American interpretations of Sino-Western relations. I begin with a consideration of the *koutou* as an emblem of the 19th-century political struggle between Great Britain and the Qing court. In the middle portion of my talk, I will address the Qianlong letter as an embodiment of traditional Chinese foreign relations and hence a key document in the tribute system interpretation of those relations. At the end of my talk, I want to return to the Qianlong letter and discuss it in relation to the reports and imperial instructions that surround the management and handling of the 'ingenious articles' offered to the emperor by the Macartney embassy.

In the Euro-American sources consulted here, I pay particular attention to the refiguring of the Qianlong letter and the *koutou* over time — for what interests me in the first part of this talk is not so much the meanings that might be ascribed to either the letter or the act in China, but what they have meant in Europe and America.[1] In this sense, much of the historical significance of these objects resides in the fact that they authorize certain assumptions about the China visited by Lord Macartney. It was, for example, despotic or autocratic, jealous or sino-centric, isolated and exclusionary, aloof and haughty. The letter and the *koutou* have often served as empirical evidence to support these characterizations of late imperial China.

Yet it is also important to note that their careers hardly run parallel to each other. The letter, for instance, is virtually absent from 19th-century western accounts of relations with China, only appearing in print, it would seem, with E. H. Parker's 1896 publication of a version found in the *Donghua lu*. The *koutou*, on the other hand, is omnipresent in 19th-century English language sources on China. In fact, it would be quite an accomplishment, I suspect, to find among these writings one that does not mention the *koutou*. Indeed, by the 1840s it had become so thoroughly fetishized[2] by western observers that former American president John Quincy Adams claimed that it, rather than opium, was the real cause of the first Anglo-Chinese war.[3]

---

[1] I am now writing on the *koutou* in China. Rather than treating it as an essentialized characteristic of imperial Chinese culture, I deal with it as one of an ensemble of bodily practices deployed in the ritual constitution of imperial sovereignty. See Hevia, 1991.

[2] I think it proper to refer to the *koutou* as a western fetish object, one that was constructed on the colonial divide. In using the term to refer to a Euro-American demonization of a Chinese practice, I follow Pietz, 1985 on the fetish.

[3] Adams' aversion to ceremonial practices such as the *koutou* might also have been inherited. His father, while American ambassador to England, argued that the business of diplomacy was submerged in ceremonial practice throughout Europe, see C. F. Adams,

THE FIRST BRITISH EMBASSY IN 19TH- AND 20TH-CENTURY LITERATURE ON CHINA

From the Macartney Embassy to the Anglo-Chinese War

Let me turn now to assessments of the embassy prior to the first Opium War, beginning with those made around the time of Macartney's return to England. It was generally assumed by the British government that it had been a success, albeit limited. The court in Beijing now had a more accurate view of English national character and Great Britain's position in the world, one of the goals of Macartney and Dundas. It had also made certain concessions concerning trade at Canton and Macartney had been able to acquire and ship to India tea plants, mulberry trees, and silkworm cocoons. He had also negotiated an audience protocol that not only avoided the *koutou* but introduced aspects of European practices into Chinese court ceremony. His success on this count demonstrated what would become for Macartney's diplomatic successors the chief lesson of the embassy: when met with firmness, China's 'immutable laws' were alterable.

Although public praise of the embassy was somewhat muted following Macartney's return to England, it became an accepted judgement, especially after the publications of several accounts by members of the embassy, that it had if nothing else greatly enhanced knowledge about China.[1] Some went even further. As late as 1836, an authoritative source such as John Francis Davis still gave the embassy high marks and argued that the conditions of trade had improved at Canton as a result of Macartney's judicious diplomacy. But Davis' view was increasingly a minority one, especially after the debacle of the Amherst embassy, the abolition of the East India Company monopoly, the shrill parliamentary lobbying of free-traders such as James Matheson (1836), and the comedy of chairs that represented, to quote John Quincy Adams, Napier's 'melancholy catastrophe' at Canton (1910: 305).[2]

Much more common by the 1830s were notions that regardless of what actions ambassadors performed before the Chinese emperor conditions of

---

1853, 8: 251–259. At the same time, in some circles in England, court ceremony became an object of mockery in the early 19th-century. See for example Macauley's remarks on ceremony cited in Crosby, 1991 and Thackery, 1991: 13.

[1] The idea that the only thing the embassy accomplished was to increase knowledge about China has been a recurrent theme in evaluations of it. See, for example, Dulles, 1930: 141.

[2] For an interesting revisionist account of these events, see Ch'un, 1984.

diplomacy and trade would remain the same. Nothing short of force would alter Chinese jealousy and exclusionism. China was increasingly characterized as a despotic regime in which wealth and commerce were held in contempt and for which, to quote Hugh Murray, 'ancient usages' such as the *koutou* were the very 'soul' of government (1836, 2: 161–164).[1] In this atmosphere, the Macartney embassy was a futile exercised summed up best perhaps in the following epigram of 1834.

> It has justly been observed, that the ambassador was received with the utmost politeness, treated with the utmost hospitality, watched with the utmost vigilance and, dismissed with the utmost civility.[2]

John Quincy Adams' Defence of British Policy

What these new assessments of the embassy point to, particularly in the context of growing tensions and more aggressive British action in China, is an interpretative shift and a re-historicization of intercourse between China and Great Britain. Where Macartney saw ceremony as negotiable and Bonaparte later argued that embassies to China ought to comply with local customs because even in Europe a distinction was made between a sovereign and his ambassador (Rockhill, 1905: 37–38), critics increasingly drew attention to 'laws of nature' and 'laws of nations,' both of which imposed rules of behaviour that transcended local practices.

One of the more strident advocates of this view, as I previously noted, was John Quincy Adams. Adams publicly justified British aggression before the Massachusetts Historical Society in 1840, so disturbing the editor of the *North American Review* that the latter refused to publish the written version of the address.[3] According to Adams, China had no right to close itself off from the rest of the world, by which he seems to have meant Christian European nations. In shutting out European trade and enclosing themselves behind high walls of exclusion, the Chinese violated the law of nations that

[1] In this argument the Macartney embassy provided an authoritative source of materials on the imperial court's behaviour. Murray notes, for instance, that the British embassy received greater notice than other ambassadors who on the same day 'performed the kotou with the deepest humility' (1836, 1: 310), but still failed to accomplish anything of substance.

[2] The epigram appears in Auber, 1834: 200; Abbott, 1843: 232; Willson, 1903, 2: 323; Robbins, 1908: 461; Pritchard, 1936: 379; Cranmer-Byng, 1957–58: 183; and Hsü, 1970: 206. It was also paraphrased by Morse and MacNair, 1931: 52.

[3] In fact, while versions of it appeared in a few contemporary newspapers, the address which Adams apparently gave did not appear in print until 1910. It has been cited often, see for example Overlach, 1919: 8; Soothill, 1925: 132; Holt, 1962: 102; Hibbert, 1970: 377.

imposed a 'moral obligation' for commercial intercourse. Such obligations were, in turn, rooted for Adams in '*Laws* of Nature' and 'Nature's *God*.' Put in these metaphysical terms, Adams was then able to locate the real scandal of the *koutou* — it was only natural law and God, he said, 'to which we [i. e., citizens of Christian nations] bow the knee ...' (1910: 305). China's 'arrogant and insupportable' pretension that it could hold intercourse with others on the basis of an 'insulting and degrading' act only proper to relations between lord and vassal was, Adams concluded, the sole cause of the war, not opium.

By presenting his justifications for British actions in China in these terms, Adams enunciated a North Atlantic diplomatic consensus with universalist pretensions, one that became increasingly impatient with what its advocates saw as the backward practices of the rest of the world. Adams defines, in effect, an absolute divide, a diametrical opposition, and attaches a clear name to it; one, I might add, derived from the natives themselves. The difference here is crucial and will animate many accounts of China into this century. For the point is that members of the Christian nations Adams refers to enter the realms of others on their feet and remain erect; only vassals and slaves *koutou*.

Adams' reference to the 'arrogant and insupportable pretension' of China's leaders also might serve as a kind of refrain justifying increasingly aggressive Euro-American penetration of China over the second half of the 19th-century. The same sort of assertion is evident, for example, in Lord Elgin's lament at the time of the second opium war. In his diary he spoke of 'the painfulness of the position of a negotiator who has to treat with persons who yield nothing to reason and everything to fear, and who are at the same time profoundly ignorant of the subjects under discussion and of their own interests' (cited in A. Smith, 1901, 2: 19). Clearly open to question now was Macartney's optimism that Chinese officials could be adaptable if dealt with firmly.

These shifts in representation were also coupled with a kind of erasure of some of the physical evidence of the Macartney embassy still present in China in 1860. When British troops entered the Yuanming Gardens, they identified the carriage and cannons Macartney had presented to Qianlong. Of the carriages we hear no more, but the cannons were supposed to have been shipped back to their place of manufacture, the Woolwich Arsenal.[1]

---

[1] Published accounts of the expedition also indicate that there was an awareness that the Yuanming Gardens had significance for earlier British embassies. Garnet Wolesley, for example, referred to the gardens as the site 'in which the ambassador of an English king

The repatriation of gifts once given by George III to the Qianlong emperor might signal a new assessment of the embassy — that it was a embarrassing failure that could only be set right by British arms.

The Audience Question (1860 to 1900)

I want to turn briefly now to treatment of the Macartney embassy between the opium wars and the fall of the Qing dynasty. Two aspects of interpretation stand out. The first of these is the increasingly negative view that began to emerge among a number of writers on Anglo-Chinese and Sino-Western relations. While not viewed as disapprovingly as the Dutch embassy that followed it in 1795,[1] the Macartney embassy was criticized for having gone too far in attempting to please the Chinese court (Eames, 1909: 130). Probably the most extreme view in this regard was that of the American diplomat William Rockhill who argued in a paper which appeared in the *American Historical Review* in 1897 that substantial evidence existed indicating Macartney may have *koutou*ed before Qianlong (see 1905: 31).

The second factor in interpretation has to do with what the Rev. Arthur Smith referred to in 1901 as the 'irreconcilable controversy' over the audience question (1901, 1: 27), a controversy which was not resolved to the satisfaction of Euro-American diplomats' until the Boxer Protocol of 1901 (see Hevia, 1990). After the 1860 ratification of the Tianjin treaty at the Hall of Ceremonies (the Board of Rites or *Libu*) in the Qing capital, British officials in China, became increasingly aware of Qing audience procedures. Leading the way was Thomas Francis Wade — and this was something very new and innovative — who studied court ritual manuals, historical texts, available government documents, and ancient texts such as the *Liji, Yili* and *Zhouli*. Significantly, Wade used his knowledge of these Chinese sources in his negotiations with officials of the newly established Zongli Yamen.[2]

In these negotiations, Wade cited the Macartney embassy as a precedent. For him it demonstrated that audience procedures could and had been al-

---

had been insulted with impunity (1862: 226; also see Hevia, 1992). In addition to the official reason he gave for destroying the gardens — i. e., as 'a solemn act of retribution' for Chinese 'treachery,' perhaps these facts were also on Lord Elgin's mind.

[1] 19th- and 20th-century disparaging of the Dutch embassy was commonplace. Duyvendak set out in part to correct the record. See his 1939: 1–4 for sources that make negative evaluations of the embassy, beginning with Barrow in 1806.

[2] On the negotiations see Wade's correspondence in Public Record Office, London: Foreign Office (1839–1887), file 17 and Wang, 1971. Also see Giles, 1898, for a catalogue of Wade's library.

tered. At the same time, Wade made it clear that Euro-American diplomats were no longer willing to bend the knee as Macartney had done (Cooley, 1981: 88). Rather they wanted a ceremony consistent with European usages in which the ambassador bowed at the waist three times upon entering and leaving the presence of a foreign sovereign.[1] While a few audiences were held along these lines in subsequent years, in the view of most observers they were usually tainted by either being held in sites associated with tribute and inferiority or in buildings other than the main audience halls of the Forbidden City.[2]

Following the events in 1900, the foreign powers moved to make a final resolution to the audience question. They incorporated into the Boxer Treaty a detailed protocol for audiences. From 1901 forward they were to be held in the Qianqing Hall, the first of the innermost set of halls in the Forbidden City, where diplomats would enter through the centre door and make their three bows. In addition, audiences were to be held individually for members of the diplomatic corps when they presented their credentials or communications from their heads of state. The emperor was not to keep them waiting and he was to receive their communications in his own hands.

In the wake of these changes something rather interesting happened. From the New Year of 1902, when the protocol was first applied until the fall of the dynasty, 33 audiences for the entire diplomatic corps were held at either the Qianqing palace or the new summer palace. Even more extraordinary, during the same period I have counted 158 individual audiences held for ambassadors and visiting dignitaries.[3]

This huge increase in diplomatic audiences marked the demise of the *koutou* as a living political issue between European powers and the Qing empire. In turn, representations of the *koutou* also changed. Certainly

---

[1] Wang 1971 discusses the negotiations leading up to the audience of 1873. Little has been done on the period after this beyond Rockhill, 1905.

[2] Audiences held in 1873 and 1891 were at the Ziguangge, located to the west of the 'Forbidden City' proper, a site westerners associated with tribute and inferiority (Smith, 1901, 1: 28). However, beginning in 1894 the young Guangxu emperor shifted the audience venue to first the Chengguang hall and later the Wenhua Hall, located to the west of the Donghua Gate within the Forbidden City. There the emperor received the Russian, French, American ambassadors, accepting directly from them communications and credentials as Macartney had done; there he also received the wives of the diplomatic corps. These last two audiences occurred in 1898, the year of the *coup d'état* that ended the emperor's reformist career.

[3] There may have even been more. These figures come from printed audience notices to be found at the Qing archives in Beijing.

people still saw it as a humiliation for westerners, but some began to argue that it had other meanings for the Chinese. The Empress Dowager's portrait painter Catherine Carl argued in 1909 that the *koutou* did not 'imply any slave-like inferiority' on the performer, but was rather a 'time honored' way of expressing thanks to the sovereign (148). The popular conveyor of Qing court culture, Princess Der Ling, in one of her reminiscences entitled simply *Kowtow*, claims that her father required it of his secretary as an apology for a slanderous act committed against her (1929: 199). By the 1930s and 40s the act underwent several other transformations.

In his early discussion of it, John K. Fairbank spoke of the *koutou* as both good manners and repayment for imperial room and board (1942 and 1948, the latter interpretation he would drop from subsequent editions of his 1948). At about the same time, E. H. Pritchard published his seminal essay on the *koutou* and the Macartney embassy. While accepting Fairbank's general characterization, Pritchard went further in arguing that not only wasn't the act intended to be 'humiliating or degrading,' but that westerners had completely misconstrued its importance. Rather than being a central act of submission, Pritchard suggested that the very dispatching of embassies and participation in the embassy routine was submission. 'To refuse to kotow,' he concluded, 'after having conformed to all other parts of the suzerain-vassal relationship was in reality pointless, and grew out of a profound misunderstanding of the meaning of the act itself ...' (1943: 197–199).

What allowed both Fairbank and Pritchard to cast matters in these terms was not simply the transformation of the *koutou* from an object of political contention to an object of historical investigation. Equally significant was the fact that their revisionism relied on new conceptual apparatuses and categories emerging from fields such as sociology and cultural anthropology. For what these two scholars did was to refigure the *koutou* as a *cultural* issue located within patterns of universal historical development — that is, the *koutou* became part the cultural scheme of a pre-modern or traditional society.

At virtually the same time, influential Chinese scholars were making similar arguments. In 1936 in an address given here in London, T. F. Tsiang spoke of a tribute system, a term and a complex of practices Fairbank would soon popularize as embodying a fundamental difference to external relations between traditional China and the modern West. In this formation, the tribute system was distinctly part of the traditional world because it perpetuated hierarchical, as opposed to egalitarian, international relations.

Yet it should also be recalled that while the scholars I have just mentioned might have put a more benign face on the *koutou* for western readers, the more negative representation of the *koutou* did not disappear. There were those, in other words, who while accepting a 20th-century social systems approach, continued to treat the *koutou* as a distasteful and scandalous act typical of China's pre-modern sense of universal superiority. Fairbank himself led the way here by taking a more critical approach from the time of his *Trade and Diplomacy on the China Coast* (1953) forward, eventually characterizing the *koutou* as one of those 'rituals of abject servitude' common in traditional China (Fairbank, 1988: 14). This line of representation dovetailed in part with the English word 'kowtow,' which remains a term of derision and ridicule,[1] and gives it a history outside of its incidence as a Chinese act.

But, *koutou* had another trajectory as well, one pointed to in the critical debates of the late 1960s and early 1970s. I think here in particular of Joseph Esherick's 1972 criticism of the Harvard school historians of China. Directed especially at Fairbank and pointing to the similarity between the historiography of the Harvard school and that of John Quincy Adams discussed above, Esherick argued that Fairbank and others had constructed an elaborate apologetics for the use of force in China by western powers. In so doing these historians had failed to come to grips with the historic impact of western expansion throughout Asia. Because I too see an affinity between the views of Adams and Fairbank, I find Esherick's argument particularly compelling and well worth taking up again.

In order to do so, I would like now to turn to the letter from the Qianlong emperor to George III. It will be my basic argument that the letter acquired its contemporary significance when, after the demise of the Qing dynasty, the political conflict between the Qing and the British empires was recast as a cultural struggle, fraught with misunderstandings and misapprehensions, typical of confrontations between traditional and modern societies. In the process, the historic conflict between these two empires entered into a new narrative construct, the universal story of progress and modernization,

---

[1] Following events in Tiananmen in 1989, the *Washington Post National Weekly Edition* (December 4–10, 1989) ran the following headline — 'Will Bush Kowtow to Peking?' British newspapers have often made reference to the kowtow in their critical assessments of the government's negotiation of the Hong Kong issue. See, for example, Jonathan Mirsky, 'Major must not kowtow in Peking,' *Observer*, September 1, 1991, a piece which includes the Gillray caricature of Macartney on bent knee, 'but no more' before the Chinese emperor. As I was preparing these remarks, syndicated columnist William Safire characterized the entire Bush policy toward China as kowtowing, see the Raleigh *News and Observer*, September 15, 1992.

whose main themes included the triumph of reason and rationality over habit and customary practices.

The Qianlong Letter and the Tribute System Synthesis

For the last fifty years the tribute system synthesis, popularized by John K. Fairbank, has been the reigning interpretative framework for organizing materials about traditional Chinese foreign relations. Modern historians tell us that it was *this* system that Lord Macartney came into contact with during his embassy. Perhaps more importantly they argue that it was the persistence and inflexibility of this system that accounts for Macartney's failures.

According to Fairbank, the essential features of the tribute system evolved as a result of the success of Chinese culture in maintaining dominance over 'barbarian peoples of inferior culture.' This pattern repeated itself from the Shang dynasty until the 19th-century, when for the first time China came into contact with an 'equal civilization.' The tribute system regulated relations with border peoples, functioning to reproduce Chinese civilization and social stasis.[1] In this milieu, China's isolation from 'equal civilizations' produced 'a sense of superiority' which in turn created 'sino-centrism,' a cultural characteristic reinforced by complex dependencies in which 'barbarian' groups came to want and need the cultural goods of the Chinese empire. These wants and needs in turn functioned to transform the occasional 'barbarian' conquest dynasty into Chinese-style rulers (sinicization). The upshot was a failure to progressively rationalize on two fronts: China did not produce a body of codified international law and it failed to properly separate the economic from the cultural-symbolic.

Implicit in Fairbank's argument was another, one that appears heavily influenced by 19th- and 20th-century historiography of the 'West.' Beginning in the Roman empire, tribute had gradually given way to regularized taxation and ever-increasing economic rationality epitomized in the emergence of disinterested capitalism. Coterminous with the development of economic rationality was that of legal rationality. Here law functioned in two ways; it protected the domain of economic activity within a territorial entity and established rules of behaviour between societies, nations, cultures. None of this had happened in China; rather, the absence of external challenges had produced a kind of involution in which law and

---

[1] We should note here that terms like tradition, civilization, and culture appear interchangeably in Fairbank; and second that culture appears as both cause and effect of 'cultural particularism.'

economic activity collapsed into *culture*. The tribute system, presumably inappropriately, combined 'diplomacy' and 'trade,' while never overtly acknowledging that it was fulfilling either of these quasi-natural functions (Fairbank, 1942; Fairbank and Teng, 1941). This was because within the terms of Chinese culture there could be no true diplomacy (based as it must be on natural equality between sovereign states) and because commerce was not as highly valued as, say, farming.[1] The upshot was that an isolated China developed an entrenched culturalism, as opposed to a more modern nationalism (see Fairbank, 1942 and Fairbank, Reischauer, and Craig, 1989: 177–179), and was ill-prepared as a result to deal with the Western powers when they arrived at China's door.

It is within this interpretation that we might begin to appreciate the letter from the Qianlong emperor to George III. For what the letter seems to substantiate is the tribute system and China's traditional culturalism, nicely and conveniently compacted into one text. Of equal significance, once it is established as a characteristic feature of traditional culture, the tribute system can be dealt with in an ironic mode, deflecting attention away from Euro-American actions in China. The irony was that the same system which accounted for the survival of the Chinese world order for over 2000 years was now the cause of its downfall.

But this was only part of the strength of the tribute system approach. Where it proved most useful was in continually providing significant objects within a tradition-modernity framework for the increasingly popular multi-disciplinary comparative approach to Chinese history which took institutions as its focal point.

Let me provide one example relevant to the discussion here. In his study of Sino-Western diplomacy from 1858–1880, Immanuel Hsü, building upon the tribute system synthesis, juxtaposed *t'i-chih* (a term appearing both in the Qianlong letter and in various court records of the Macartney embassy) to the western notion of diplomatic representation and equality between states. Hsü argued that beyond its narrow sense as basic or essential institution, the word *t'i-chih* was firmly rooted in Confucianism and included 'the Chinese way of life and the proper manner of doing things from the Chinese standpoint,' something whose maintenance was a matter of

[1] To paraphrase Parsons, whose sociological categories Fairbank employed (1982:326), Chinese culture, while in some aspects providing the basis for rationality, was strongly subject to substantive rather than formal rationalization, and was shot through with particularist themes, all of which served to retard proper development (1966:77).

'prestige and face.' Hsü concluded, and I think it worth quoting him in some detail here, that *t'i-chih*:

> was in essence the Chinese counterpart of the English unwritten constitution: both being the sum total of tangible and intangible traditions, beliefs, codes, statutes, governmental systems, and religious observances. To demand of the Chinese a change in their *t'i-chih* would be tantamount to demanding of the English a change in their common law or Magna Charta ... any such amendment would be an acknowledgement of the impropriety of the Chinese system that had proved adequate for the past two thousand years (1960: 111).

Note how *t'i-chih*, much as the *koutou* before it, comes to embody the totalizing essence of the Chinese. And like the *koutou* it could stand for not only Chinese thinking about the world, but for a wide variety of practices as well. Perhaps more importantly, *t'i-chih* epitomized what Fairbank and others meant by culturalism. The Qianlong letter stands now within this framework as a manifestation of this two-thousand year old essence.

I could go on here to discuss other uses of the Macartney embassy and the Qianlong letter in tradition-modernity historiography, particularly their place in arguments that saw, to use Mark Mancall's apt phrase, the persistence of tradition in the diplomacy of the People's Republic during the 1960s.[1] Rather than doing so, however, let me elucidate a few of the problems I find with the tribute system synthesis.

First, in finding a seamless continuity across great spans of China's history, the tribute system synthesis obscures differences within that history. This is, of course, not a novel idea on my part — it has been pointed to by Rossabi and others (also see Wills, n. d. and 1984), but not, I might add, to the extent that the whole approach is questioned, only temporally modified. In other words, assumptions about the triumph of culture over rationality, for instance, remain intact even when it is argued that at certain times in Chinese history the tribute system was not in play. Second, reliance on timeless attributes of minds, whether they be Chinese minds or any others denies the potential not only for novelty and innovation, but also for substantive critiques of proposals made by European diplomats such as Lord Macartney, an example of which I shall take up in a moment. Instead, many who have followed Fairbank have argued that Chinese minds were so thoroughly conditioned by the beliefs fostered in the tribute system, beliefs which made it impossible for them to distinguish illusions from reality, that

---

[1] Mancall, 1963. Also see Fairbank, 1966 and Cranmer-Byng, 1965–66.

they were incapable of change until a massive shock on the order of Euro-American gunboat diplomacy was administered.[1] I think such arguments fairly good example of the apologetics critiqued by Esherick.

Third, and this is especially the case with both the *koutou* and the Qianlong letter, the tribute system synthesis separates these objects from their historically specific occurrences, treating them as signifiers of transcendent meaning that operate over vast stretches of time and space. I would think that we ought to be just as sceptical of such claims with respect to China as we often are when equally totalizing arguments are made about the European or American past.

Finally, while the tradition-modernity model might have a certain utility as a pedagogical device in undergraduate survey courses on East Asia, it does an excessive amount of violence to the subjects of our study. In addition to the sorts of problems associated with temporal distancing that Johannes Fabian (1983) and other critics of anthropology have pointed to, the holistic framework of tradition-modernity comparativism invariably constructs the former as the negative inversion of the latter. This not only produces a history that seems only to chronicle absences and failures,[2] it produces agents who are repeatedly judged to be inferior because their reason is always and indeed must be faulty.

A RECONSIDERATION OF THE ENGLISH GIFTS

I want to close by returning to Qianlong's letter to George III, and specifically to the line that has been prominently rendered 'we have never valued ingenious articles, nor do we have the slightest need of your Country's manufactures.' My purpose will be to reconsider the imperial court's characterization of the British gifts.

For many historians working within the tradition-modernity framework, Qianlong's reference to ingenious articles and British manufactures seems to epitomize what Cranmer-Byng and T. H. Levere have characterized as 'cultural collision.' These authors argue that the Qing court's response

---

[1] As Fairbank once put it '... the underlying weakness [of the Qing empire] was intellectual-institutional, that is, an habituated ignorance of foreign realities and a wilful refusal to take them into account. This was evidenced most notably in the purblind adherence to an imperial polity of asserted supremacy over all foreign sovereigns. Peking refused intercourse on equal terms until it was perforce extorted on unequal terms' (1976: 260).

[2] For a critique of this approach in the historiography of China see March, 1974: 9.

graphically demonstrates the great divide between Chinese cultural attitudes and values and those of the West. The difference, they argue, was a crucial one, for it indicated the inability of Chinese culture, and I quote them, 'to appreciate the intellectual and theoretical content of natural philosophy, with its potentially enormously useful application' (1981: 518).

In these terms, Qianlong's comments were not simply a refusal of commercial exchange or diplomatic intercourse, but of the very essence of what the embassy represented — enlightenment Europe. At the same time, however, the failure of the embassy was not only inevitable and predictable, but, as Cranmer-Byng has stressed more than once, pre-determined (Cranmer-Byng, 1957–58: 133–138 and 1962: 337).

When the dominant interpretations are cast in these apocalyptic terms, offering an alternative explanation for the content of Qianlong's letter poses a formidable challenge. I want to take it up on this occasion by considering one of the most intensely discussed subjects in the published and unpublished court records of the embassy — the handling, transport, and setting up of the English gifts. These are the things to which Qianlong seems to be referring to in his letter to George III.[1]

Any re-reading of the letter and re-consideration of the gift question would have to acknowledge that we are dealing here with a Manchu emperor and court of broad experience in forging relations with other kings and their kingdoms. And second, that what concerned these men was not necessarily China, but the Manchu empire, an empire that under Qianlong had been vastly extended and of which China made up only one, albeit the richest, part. Perhaps the Manchu emperor and his advisors did give an impression of being superior, but if so, the reason for such an attitude ought to have been understandable to the leadership of expansionist European states.

When Macartney arrived aboard the *Lion* at Tianjin in the first week of August 1793, he was asked by court officials to provide a list of the gifts. While this was normal procedure, the officials seem to have been especially keen in this instance because the vast majority of the gifts were crated and could not be seen by them. They were also receiving instructions from the emperor for particulars — dimensions, time needed for assembly as well as what they were — so that preparations could be made for their reception in Rehe, where the emperor was.

---

[1] A similar phrase is to be found in a poem the emperor is said to have written for the occasion of the Macartney audience at Rehe. See Cranmer-Byng and Levere, 1981: 520. This is the same poem to be found on the tapestry at National Maritime Museum, Greenwich.

When these questions were put to the British ambassador, his reported response was that it would take a month or more to set up some of the gifts and that once assembled, they could not be taken apart. In edicts of early August, 1793 the Qianlong emperor commented that these claims were exaggerations, an effort on Macartney's part to boast about the ingeniousness of British artisans. If it took a month to set them up, Qianlong noted, they must have taken years to manufacture in the first place. Moreover, given the claims made by Macartney, it might be extremely inconvenient and perhaps impossible to have all the gifts sent to Rehe for the emperor's birthday in mid-September. At that point a decision was made to send only smaller items to Rehe and have the rest sent to the Yuanming gardens, where the emperor, if he wished, could view them later.

All of this discussion went on without anyone on the court's side having seen the gifts. On August 20, the day before the embassy and gifts arrived at the Yuanming Yuan, the emperor made this observation:

> When the planetarium was manufactured in England and its assembly complete, it was necessary to pack it and move it around for shipment. If after assembly, they were unable to dismantle it, how were they able to pack it in separate crates, load it aboard ship, transfer it to smaller boats, and transport it overland to Beijing?

He concluded, therefore, that the ambassador's boasts had understandably misled court officers accompanying him. As a result, it was important for those responsible for the gifts to make certain that the missionaries and artisans in the emperor's service observed fully the uncrating and assembly of the larger items (*ZGCB*, 7: 42b–43b), because if in fact they could not be dismantled after assembly, how, the emperor wondered, could they be accepted (*ZGCB*, 7:45b)?[1]

Within a few days, however, Macartney was taken to the Yuanming Yuan and matters seem to have reached a resolution. The reason for this, the emperor pointed out, was that now that Macartney had seen the hall where the gifts were to be displayed and the emperor's own experts had seen the things, Macartney could no longer make extravagant claims about the size and complexity of the gifts (*ZGCB*, 7:45b–46a). The upshot of this partic-

---

[1] Two days later, the Grand Council sent a directive to the imperial commissioner Zhengrui emphasizing the emperor's concerns and adding that a detailed plan should be drawn up showing specifically the placement of the items in the halls in question. The directive also made reference to the court's understanding of the future dates of the embassy's movements and when they expected Zhengrui to memorialize on the progress of affairs, *ZGCB*, 7, 44a–44b).

ular dialogue between the emperor, court officials, and Macartney was the conclusion that the British ambassador, unlike his sincere (*cheng*) and loyal (*zhi*) sovereign, was boastful (*xuan*), arrogant (*jingao*), and ignorant (*wuzhi*).

It is here, I would suggest, in these practical issues surrounding the handling, assembly, and future disposition of the British gifts, perhaps more than any where else in the records of the embassy, that the emperor and his close advisors began to have doubts about the intentions of the British embassy. It is here also that language similar to the wording of Qianlong's letter to George III first appears. Recalling that the emperor had not yet seen the gifts it seems to me to make more sense to consider his reply not as some timeless attitude of traditional Chinese culture, but as a specific response to events going on right then in the embassy. Perhaps this was why Macartney was taken on an extensive tour of the palaces in Rehe, shown a profusion of European spheres, orreries, clocks, and musical automatons, and told that this was only one portion of the emperor's collection of such devices. The ambassador commented, in fact, 'that our presents must shrink from the comparison and 'hide their diminished heads'' (Cranmer-Byng, 1963: 125). Macartney's signs of modesty at this point appear, however, to have come too late to actually affect the court's evaluation of his character. In edicts to jurisdictions responsible for the present and future care of the embassy and in his letters to George III, the Qianlong emperor was careful to distinguish the British ambassador and his claims about the gifts from the otherwise sincerely loyal king of England.[1] This necessarily

---

[1] The question that lingers for us, however, is whether Macartney was in fact so tactless in his dealings with court officials to elicit these conclusions about his character. There is no question that Macartney was proud of the objects he was presenting. In the gift list he had made a point of emphasizing that he was not offering 'trifles of momentary curiosity but little use' (Cranmer-Byng and Levere, 1981: 523). But this hardly seems sufficient cause for the court's appraisal. On the other hand, an incident that occurred after the embassy returned to the Yuanming Yuan from Rehe may shed some light. Under a diary entry of October 1 Macartney records that court officials were encouraging a speedy completion to the work of setting up the gifts. When told that more time was needed, the officials were incredulous. Observing how ignorant they were in such matters, Macartney compared the incident to one that had occurred before his departure to Rehe. He writes that Zhengrui:

> testified no less surprise upon a former occasion, on being told that it would take several weeks to combine all the different movements of the planetarium, imagining that labour, not skill, was the only thing necessary, and that putting together so complicated a machine as a system of the universe was an operation almost as simple as the winding up a jack (Cranmer-Byng, 1963: 145–146).

brief review of the court record provides one kind of explanation for problems surrounding the gifts. But there are other ways of approaching this issue as well. For example, rather than focusing on relations between the Qing empire and Great Britain, we might consider what the British embassy tells us about the fashioning of the multi-ethnic Manchu empire and its relations to other kingdoms around it.

I have argued elsewhere that Manchu overlords fashioned imperial sovereignty through rituals that included the powers of others in their rulership. With respect to the multitude of lords in the world, the Qing court encompassed their specific and local powers in a relationship that acknowledged the Manchu king as supreme lord (*huangdi*) and other kings as loyal inferiors (*fanwang*, Hevia, 1989 and 1990). In this regard, it is important to draw attention to the fact that George III's gifts were not rejected, but rather accepted and positioned in relation to the gifts of other West Ocean kingdoms. As a result, George III was placed as a responsible sublord who was engaged with the supreme lord, the Qianlong emperor, in world-ordering cosmic and political processes.

How was it possible, one might wonder, for the gifts brought by Macartney to participate in the production of Manchu kingship? To begin, the word I translate here as gifts is, of course, *gong*, which is usually rendered as 'tribute.'[1] Regardless of how *gong* is translated, the fundamental issue, I think, is how it was connected to the construction of imperial sovereignty. In Qing imperial records I am familiar with, especially ritual texts such as the *Comprehensive Rites of the Great Qing* (*Da Qing tongli*), *gong* may be glossed as *fangwu*, local products.[2] *Fangwu* included things from other kingdoms as well as those from the imperial domain. But in the specific case of peripheral lords who wished to forge a relationship with the Manchu overlord, the prefatory comments in the *Guest Ritual* section of the *Comprehensive Rites* indicate that they were to offer the 'most precious things' of the domain they commanded to the supreme lord.

Perhaps this was the attitude reported to the emperor, one that exhibited a self-assured superiority in English skills and knowledge, one that was predisposed to believe that the complex scientific devices would somehow awe and impress the court.

[1] For a variety of reasons, not the least of which is the connotation that late 18th-century China was somehow caught up in a stage of universal historical development previously transcended by western European states, I prefer not to use the term tribute.

[2] In a variety compounds it often indicated the best of something (*gongcha*), a senior group of officials (*gongsheng*), and in the compound *gongyuan*, the provincial examination hall.

Gong, therefore, signifies a) things brought to fruition as a result of the virtuous actions of a lord in his kingdom; b) the lords ability to recognise these things as such; and c) his reverent offering of them up to the emperor. Put another way, local products embodied all the attributes of a sub-lord I have just mentioned and could therefore be interpreted by the court as signs of sincere loyalty. *Gong*, however, is only one part of the picture. If the offerings of a sub-lord *open* the process of encounter between the Manchu court and other kingdoms, what brings the process to *completion* are the emperor's bestowals (ci) and rewards ($shang$) to his sincerely loyal inferior. And like those things offered up, the downward flow is also made up of precious things, things that the emperor commands in his own kingdom.

It is important, however, not to confuse this process of exchange, if it may even be called that, with familiar categories generated from the tradition-modernity model. I do not think it helpful to think of these precious things as payment because it enmeshes them in forms of value which seem to me highly inappropriate (market exchange value or utilitarian value for instance). Nor do I think it especially helpful to characterize them as symbolic, because that interpretation tends to separate them from the specificities of their production, while stabilizing their meaning in such a way that literally no more can be said about them. (I might add parenthetically that for those who doubt me on this point, I would refer them to the use of the term symbolic in the context of 'traditional Chinese foreign relations.' It tends to conclude, rather than begin discussion, because, after all, we are thought to be dealing with the *merely* symbolic, the *merely* ceremonial. The real action and meanings of embassies, as we learn within the tribute system synthesis, lie elsewhere).

On the other hand, if we take the construction of *gong* in terms I have just outlined, one observation comes readily to mind. Recall Macartney's sightseeing at Rehe. Might not one purpose have been to show him that the British gifts were indistinguishable from objects the court already had? Might not part of the difficulty have been that there was no way to clearly link the things presented by Macartney with George III's dextrous and virtuous management of his kingdom? Put another way, if *gong* offerings were held to embody the specific kingship of a loyal sub-lord, wouldn't the similarity of the British gifts to other European items in the emperor's possession, and Macartney's claims about their special virtue have been a diplomatic blunder?

Such questions suggest to me that perhaps there was more going on in encounters like the Macartney embassy than either the economic or symbolic interpretation of *gong* can accommodate. One example of such excess is suggested in an observation made some years ago by Cranmer-Byng. He noted that the court's bestowals to the British included Korean and 'Mohammaden patterned cloth,' and perhaps even Indian linen; and concluded that it is interesting to know 'tribute once given might be distributed to other tributary states ...' (1957–58: 166).

I fully concur. For what Cranmer-Byng's observation directs our attention to are issues surrounding the handling, storage, and the re-circulation of *gong*, a subject we know far too little about. It also suggests, for example, that the ability to gather in the things of one sub-lord and bestow them on another might be a central instantiation of imperial power. In this respect, it might be useful to think about the role of objects in the making of a universal moral order; that is, in the construction of Manchu imperial hegemony.

Finally, we may wonder too about the circulation within the imperial family of objects presented by other lords. I raise this issue because of a conversation I had with Evelyn Rawski while preparing this discussion. In her ongoing study of the imperial family, Rawski has come across gift exchange lists of enormous size and regularity in the imperial archives at Beijing. They indicate the movement of Buddhist objects such as images, paintings, models of mandalas, etc. from Mongol Khans and Buddhist hierarchs to the court, where they were circulated and exchanged among members of the imperial clan. Precisely what conclusions can be drawn from this particular form of *gong* remains to be seen. At present, however, these various facets of gift exchange suggest that we might be particularly attentive to those signifying practices which involved relationships between people and objects. For it was in and through practices like those I have reviewed here that a complex agent, the Manchu imperial court, was produced and reproduced, and Manchu overlordship in eastern Asia extended into the future.

REFERENCES

Abbott, Jacob. 1843. *China and the English, or the Character and Manner of the Chinese as Illustrated in the History of their Intercourse with Foreigners.* New York: William Holdredge.

Adams, Charles F., ed. 1853. *The Works of John Adams.* Boston: Little, Brown, and Company.

Adams, John Q. 1909–1910. 'J. Q. Adams on the Opium War'. *Proceedings of the Massachusetts Historical Society* 43: 295–324.

Auber, Peter. 1834. *China*. London: Partbury, Allen Co.

Barrow, John. 1806. *Travels in China*. London: T. Cadell.

Carl, Katherine. 1907. *With the Empress Dowager of China*. New York: Century Co.

Ch'un, Allen. 1984. 'The Meaning of Crisis and the Crisis of Meaning in History: An Interpretation of the Anglo-Chinese Opium War'. *Bulletin of the Institute of Ethnology, Academia Sinica,* 55 (Spring): 169–228.

Cooley, James. 1981. *T. F. Wade in China*. Leiden: E. J. Brill.

Cranmer-Byng, J. L., ed. *An Embassy to China*. Hamden, CN.: Archon Books.

_____. 1965–66. 'The Chinese Attitude Towards External Relations'. *International Journal* 21, 1: 57–77.

_____. 1957–1958. 'Lord Macartney's Embassy to Peking in 1793: From Official Chinese Documents'. *J. of Oriental Studies* 4, 1–2: 117–85.

_____ and T. H. Levere. 1981. 'A Case Study in Cultural Collision: Scientific Apparatus in the Macartney Embassy to China, 1793'. *Annals of Science* 38: 503–525.

Crosby, Christina. 1991. *The Ends of History: Victorians and 'the woman question'*. London: Routledge.

DQTL. Da Qing tongli. 1883 reprint of 1824 re-edited edition. Beijing: Palace Edition.

Davis, John F. 1836. *The Chinese: A General Description of the Empire and Its Inhabitants*. London: Charles Knight. 2 vols.

Der Ling. 1929. *Kowtow*. New York: Dodd, Mead & Co.

Dulles, Foster Rhea. 1930. *The Old China Trade*. Boston: Houghton Mifflin.

Duyvendak, J. J. L. 1939. 'The Last Dutch Embassy to the Chinese Court'. *T'oung Pao* 34.1–2: 1–116.

Eames, James B. 1909. *The English in China*. Reprint ed. New York: Barnes and Noble Books, 1974.

Esherick, Joseph. 1972. 'Harvard on China: The Apologetics of Imperialism'. *Bulletin of Concerned Asian Scholars* 4.4: 9–16.

Fabian, Johannes. 1983. *Time and the Other*. New York: Columbia U. P.

Fairbank, John K. 1942. 'Tributary Trade and China's Relations with the West'. *The Far Eastern Quarterly* 1: 129–149.

_____. 1948 (1958, 1971, 1979). *The United States and China.* Cambridge, Ma.: Harvard U. P.

_____. 1953. *Trade and Diplomacy on the China Coast.* Stanford: Stanford U. P.

_____. 1966. 'China's World Order: The Tradition of Chinese Foreign Relations'. *Encounter* (December): 14–20.

_____. 1976. 'The Creation of the Treaty System', 213–263. In J. K. Fairbank, ed. *The Cambridge History of China: Late Ch'ing 1800–1911* 10.1. London: Cambridge U. P.

_____. 1982. *China Bound: A Fifty Year Memoir.* New York: Harper & Row.

_____. 1988. 'Born Too Late'. *New York Review of Books.* 35, 2 (February 18).

_____ and S. Y. Teng. 1941. 'On the Ch'ing Tributary System'. *Harvard Journal of Asiatic Studies* 6:135–246.

_____. 1954 (1975). *China's Response to the West.* New York: Atheneum.

_____, E. O. Reischauer, and A. M. Craig. 1978. *East Asia: Tradition and Transformation.* Boston: Houghton Mifflin Company.

Giles, Herbert. 1898. *A Catalogue of the Wade Collection of the Chinese and Manchu Books in the Library of the U. of Cambridge.* Cambridge: The U. P.

Hevia, James L. 1989. 'A Multitude of Lords: Qing Court Ritual and the Macartney Embassy of 1793'. *Late Imperial China* 10.2: 72–105.

_____. 1990. 'Making China "Perfectly Equal"'. *Journal of Historical Sociology* 3.4: 380–401.

_____. 1991. 'Sovereignty and Subject: Constructing Relations of Power in Qing Imperial Ritual'. In Angela Zito and Tani Barlow, eds. *Body, Subjectivity, and Power in China.* Forthcoming U. of Chicago P.

_____. 1992. 'Loot's Fate: The Economy of Plunder and the Moral Life of Objects "From the Summer Palace of the Emperor of China"'. Association of Asian Studies Annual Meeting, Washington, DC, April.

Hibbert, Christopher. 1970. *The Dragon Wakes: China and the West, 1793–1911.* New York: Harper & Row.

Holt, Edgar. 1964. *The Opium Wars in China.* London: Putnam.

Hsü, Immanuel C. Y. 1960. *China's Entrance into the Family of Nations: The Diplomatic Phase, 1858–1880.* Cambridge, Ma.: Harvard U. P.

_____. 1970, 1990. *The Rise of Modern China.* New York and London: Oxford.

Mancall, M. 1963. 'The Persistence of Tradition in Chinese Foreign Policy'. *Annals of the American Academy of Political and Social Science* 349: 14–26.

March, Andrew. 1974. *The Idea of China.* New York: Praeger.

Matheson, James. 1836. *The Present Position and Prospects of the British Trade with China.* London: Smith, Elder, and Co.

Morse, H. B. and MacNair, H. F. 1931. *Far Eastern International Relations.* New York: Russell & Russell. 2 vol.

Murray, Hugh et al. 1836. (1843) *An Historical and Descriptive Account of China.* London: Simplin, Marshall, & Co. 3 vol.

Overlach, Theodore. 1919. *Foreign Financial Control in China.* Reprint ed. New York: Arno P., 1976.

Parker, E. H. 1896. 'From the Emperor of China to King George the Third'. *Nineteenth Century* (July): 45–54.

Parsons, Talcott. 1966. *Societies.* Englewood Cliffs, N. J.: Prentice Hall.

Pietz, William. 1985. 'The Problem of the Fetish, I'. *Res* 9: 5–17.

Pritchard, E. H. 1936. *The Crucial Years of Anglo-Chinese Relations.* Pullman, Wa.: Research Studies of the State College of Washington 4:3–4

_____. 1943. 'The Kowtow in the Macartney Embassy to China in 1793'. *Far Eastern Quarterly* 2, 2: 163–201.

Public Record Office, London.

Robbins, Helen M. 1908. *Our First Ambassador to China: An Account of the Life of George, Earl of Macartney.* London: John Murray.

Rockhill, William W. 1905. *Diplomatic Audiences at the Court of China.* Reprint ed. Taipei: Ch'eng-wen Publishing Co.

Rossabi, Morris, ed. 1983. *China Among Equals.* Berkeley: U. of California P.

Rozman, Gilbert, ed. 1981. *The Modernization of China.* New York: Free Press.

Russell, Bertrand. 1922. *The Problem of China.* London: George Allen & Unwin.

Soothill, W. E. 1925. *China and the West: A Sketch of Their Intercourse.* Reprint ed. San Francisco: Chinese Materials Center, Inc., 1975

Smith, Arthur. 1901. *China in Convulsion.* New York: Fleming H. Revell. 2 vol.

Spence, Jonathan. 1990. *In Search of Modern China.* New York: W. W. Norton.

Staunton, George L. 1797. *An Authentic Account of an Embassy from the King of Great Britain to the Emperor of China.* London: G. Nichol. 2 vols.

Thackeray, William M. 1991. *The History of Henry Esmond, Esq.* Edited by Donald Hawes. Oxford: Oxford U. P.

Tsiang, T. F. 1936. 'China and European Expansion'. *Politica* 2: 1–18.

Wang, Tseng-tsai. 1971. 'The Audience Question: Foreign Representatives and the Emperor of China, 1858–1873'. *Historical Journal* 14.3: 617–633.

Wills, John E., Jr. 1984. *Embassies & Illusions: Dutch and Portuguese Envoys to K'ang-hsi, 1666–1687.* Cambridge, Ma.: Harvard U. P.

_____. n. d. 'Continuities and Transformations in the History of Chinese Foreign Relations: A Review Article'. Unpublished paper.

Willson, Beckles. 1903. *Ledger and Sword.* London: Longmans, Green, and Co.

Wolseley, Garnet. 1862. *Narrative of the War with China in 1860.* Wilmington, De.: Scholarly Resources.

ZGCB. Zhanggu congbian. 1928–30. (Collected Historical Documents). Beijing: Palace Museum.

HISTORY, LEGEND AND TREATY PORT IDEOLOGY, 1925–1931

ROBERT A. BICKERS

I WOULD LIKE TODAY to discuss the use of history by the non-missionary treaty port communities in China in the later 1920s, that is the interpretations of the history of Sino-British relations preferred and the choice of events commonly referred to. It deals with a few of the themes which pervade treaty port writings and the discourse revealed in public debates and in private papers during the years of upheaval in the foreign communities between the May 30th shootings in 1925 and the Japanese invasion of Manchuria in September 1931. As will be shown even such distant events as the Macartney embassy were the subject of live debate.

The treaty port communities required, as all communities do, legends to bolster their technical legitimacy and define themselves. These legends formed an important part of the ideas transmitted during the socialisation of Britons arriving in the treaty port communities.[1] They were passed on to new arrivals as justifications, both of their presence in China and of their continued right to stay there in the face of Chinese nationalism. These historical, and contemporary, legends were widely transmitted, orally in the club bars and dinner parties that marked out the social round of treaty port life, through newspapers and magazine articles, through histories of the foreign presence written by treaty port residents and also through fictions such as those by James Bennett, Dorothy Graham, Alice Tisdale Hobart and Bertram Lenox Simpson.[2]

---

[1] For an account of socialisation in the British treaty port communities see R. A. Bickers, 'Changing British Attitudes to China and the Chinese, 1928–1931', Unpublished Ph. D. thesis, School of Oriental and African Studies, University of London, 1992, pp. 77–122.

[2] *Oriental Affairs*, a Shanghai-based British-edited news magazine reprinted excerpts from Hunter's *The Fankwae at Canton* in 1937 and it was common to find in it articles, for example, on 'Jesuits at the Court of Peking', 'A Forgotten British Embassy — Colonel Charles Cathcart' or 'Shanghai's Cemeteries and Monuments: History Engraved on Stone', *Oriental Affairs*, 1935–1941, passim. For fictions see, for example, Dorothy Graham, *The China Venture* (London, 1929); Alice Tisdale Hobart, *Pidgin Cargo* (London, 1929); Veronica and Paul King, *The Commissioner's Dilemma: An International Tale of the China of Yesterday* (London, 1929), forward.

The attitudes acquired and bolstered in this socialisation militated against Britons adopting anything but a hostile attitude towards the diplomatic concessions necessitated by the victory of the *Guomindang* in 1927. The privileges, and indeed the livelihoods, of the majority of treaty port Britons were widely thought to depend on the perpetuation of the unequal relationship with the Chinese founded on the treaties of the previous century and the structures of informal empire. The direct influence of treaty port residents on the diplomatic process is questionable. Their ability to inflame the situation indubitable. A clear examination of treaty port ideology is, therefore, necessary. The following is a tentative sketch of the main themes to be found. Treaty port ideology was more than just imperial thinking with local characteristics. It had a life of its own and sought for its legitimacy within the whole scope of its own history, from the Macartney mission to the Nanjing Incident of 1927.

THE CANON

Principal among these interpretations of the history of the treaty ports was what can only be described by the neologism 'mudflat-ism'; that is the common belief that the treaty ports and concessions had been mud flats or marshes before the arrival of the Europeans. This, while usually technically true carried the implied and frequently explicit gloss that the Europeans had been solely responsible for constructing the successful ports and industries of modernising China. It also suggested that the continued foreign presence was vital to the economic health of the country.[1]

The myth of quick money and easy living in China was still strong. Certainly fortunes were made in China and the obituarists and leader writers on the *North China Daily News* never let people forget this. 'Rags to riches' (and thence to charity) stories were the stuff of the legends by which the foreign community characterized itself.[2] This myth often merged with sentimental accounts of the advantages of treaty port living. It was compounded by the sense of isolation in the smaller British communities, and by perceived racial threats, especially during the May 30th boycott move-

---

[1] *North China Herald* [*NCH*], 3/3/28, p. 336; F. L. Hawks Pott, *A Short History of Shanghai: Being an Account of the Growth and Development of the International Settlement* (Shanghai, 1928), p. 1; Rodney Gilbert, *What's Wrong with China* (London, 1926), p. 291; W. E. Soothill, *China and England* (London, 1928), pp. 61–85; *Directory and Chronicle of China and Japan ... 1932* (Hong Kong, 1932), p. 858; R. d'Auxion De Ruffé, *Is China Mad?* (Shanghai, 1928), pp. 259–60; War Office, *Notes on Shanghai* (London, 1928), pp. 6, 16.

[2] 'A Great Romance of Shanghai: Death of a Resident who once Slept on the Bund and Who Gave £50,000 to a Museum', *NCH*, 21/4/28, p. 104.

ment and subsequent events. For one British Shanghai policeman Zhenjiang in 1925 was:

> (like Foochow) a glimpse of the 'good old China' of the earlier White men, when lavish ... hospitality was the keynote of everything. In olden days in ports like this the foreigner did very little work ... made money easily and spent it easily.[1]

This had a diminishing basis in reality, (there were 85 unemployed Shanghai Britons registered as searching for work in August 1932[2]) but it appears to have influenced the behaviour and motivations of many people.

Within the British communities there were other more practical unifying legends. The Britons lionized in China were not the Jardines, Dents, Keswicks or Swires, whose activities had established the British in China, but the imperialists such as General Gordon (after whom the headquarters of the Tientsin British Municipal Council was named) and Sir Harry Parkes and Robert Hart, both of whose statues stood on the Shanghai Bund. These business communities saw their forebears then not as men of trade but as men of war and Empire, not as men who cooperated with the Chinese but as men who fought them, advised them, saved them and organized them in such a way as benefited the foreign powers.[3]

Key events in this imperial history included the foreign presence in the Qing anti-Taiping armies, the 1854 'Battle of the Muddy Flats' which marked the foundation of the Shanghai Volunteer Corps [SVC], and the Boxer battles.[4] The 1926 Wanxian Incident was immediately portrayed by the treaty port press as a British military victory solidly within this tradition

---

[1] Tinkler papers, Letter to Edith 16/12/25. Sir Eric Teichman described treaty port life as 'cheap and easy living, with the good natured and industrious Chinese always at beck and call', *Affairs of China* (London, 1938), pp. 138–39; 282.

[2] *NCH*, 3/8/32, pp. 165, 178.

[3] O. M. Green, *The Foreigner in China* (London, 1943), pp. 111–26; O. D. Rasmussen, *Tientsin: An Illustrated Outline History* (Tianjin, 1925), pp. 113–27; C. A. Montalto de Jesus' *Historic Shanghai* (Shanghai, 1909), is dedicated to Gordon; F. Maze's papers are replete with his idolisation of Hart, Maze papers, SOAS; see also his subordinate S. Wright's *Hart and the Chinese Customs* (Belfast, 1950), esp. pp. xiii–xv. An exception is the work officially sponsored by the SMC, G. Lanning and S. Couling, *The History of Shanghai, Part 1* (Shanghai, 1921), pp. 459–71, The Gordon industry was still in action in 1933 when B. M. Allen's *Gordon in China* was published in London recounting: 'one of the most dramatic pages in English history, while the cruel cunning of his Chinese colleagues serves to bring out the unselfish heroism of the young English commander', p. vi.

[4] On the role played by the formation of the SVC and the Battle of Muddy Flat in Shanghai mythology see, for example, Pott, *Short History of Shanghai*, pp. 26–30, .

of imperial militarism.[1] These beliefs had practical consequences. They provided rationales for treaty port attacks on British government policy and the activities of British officials in China.[2] It has been noted that the British Empire's heroic myths were in fact 'primarily military' and these local variants emphasized the imperial nature, and by implication importance, of the British presence in China.[3] They also reflected the fact that around a third of British males in Shanghai were involved in the Shanghai Volunteer Corps or the Police Specials. The theatre of treaty port life included a great deal of route-marching, mass inspections, military tattoos, and military funerals.[4]

THE BOXER RISING AND THE SEPOY MUTINY

The Boxer rising provided a great part of the raw material of historical debate. It was also important to the missionary community with its long professional interest in persecution and martyrdom. Many of the participants were still alive in the late 1920s. In 1924 Naval Commander, and later author, Charles Drage was entertained at dinner by Consul Sir Meyrick Hewlett's account of the Legation Siege; a young banker was also told similar first-hand stories in 1929. The treaty port press kept memories active, with articles on sites of foreign historical interest, or early European graveyards.[5] For others nationalism was 'boxerism' (heightened, fanatical, almost insane, mass anti-foreignism), especially when it was allied with anti-Christian movements. In early 1925 one naval officer recorded in his journal that: 'The trouble at Shanghai gets worse every day ... There are other serious things as well; such as anti-foreign risings in Hankow. It looks as if there might be another Boxer rising.'[6] The organisation of underground

---

[1] *The Wanhsien Epic*, reprinted from the *Central China Post* (Hankou, 1926): 'the account of a very courageous attempt on the part of a mere handful of men to rescue their fellow-countrymen and uphold the honour of the flag', enclosure, in China Letter 1129/1041/417, 17/9/26, ADM116\2497. For details of the incident itself see E. S. K. Fung, *The Diplomacy of Imperial Retreat: Britain's South China Policy, 1924–1931* (Hong Kong, 1991), p. 132.

[2] 'Our diplomats of the Victorian era were of a different mettle,' wrote 'British Trader' in the *North China Daily News* [*NCDN*], 15/8/27, p. 4.

[3] John M. Mackenzie, 'Heroic Myths of Empire', John M. Mackenzie, ed., *Popular Imperialism and the Military* (Manchester, 1992), pp. 113, 134.

[4] Bickers, 'Changing British Attitudes', pp. 104–105.

[5] Imperial War Museum, C. H. Drage papers, Journal, 24/9/24; B. C. Allan, Narrative, 11/5/63, Hong Kong and Shanghai Bank Archives, S16.1 Personal Narratives; on the press see, for example, the articles on 'British Memorials in Peking' in *NCDN*, 13/8/27, p. 11; ibid., 15/8/27, p. 7.

[6] Imperial War Museum, Simms papers, Journal, 17/1/25, see also 2/6/25. B. L. Simpson ('Putnam Weale') put forward this connection in his *Why China Sees Red* (New

communist movements also struck some observers as being as secretive and fanatical as the Boxers were supposed to have been.

A modernised version of the Boxer 'outrages' may be seen in reactions to, and the totemic use of, the Nanjing Incident in March 1927. When the National Revolutionary Army occupied the city several foreigners were killed and others only rescued after an American warship laid down an artillery barrage to cover them.[1] It also arose during the publicity generated by the case of John Thorburn, a young Briton who went missing near Shanghai in 1931 and who was later found to have been summarily executed in Chinese military custody having fatally shot two policemen:

> Are there any indications that these ancient people warped by centuries of custom and prejudice have in less than a generation changed their hearts, have they become more civilised or milder in their disposition?

asked the proposer of a motion at a public meeting of British residents in Tianjin which was called to censure the Legation for inactivity over the matter.[2]

History was resorted too for other proofs: as the Chinese were held to be characteristically cruel, opponents of the rendition of extraterritoriality claimed it would lead to a repetition of the judicial cruelties inflicted on Britons in the years before 1842 (which were often itemised in commentaries to emphasize this point).[3] The appeal to history was often based on assumptions of the unchangeability and consequent predictability of the Chinese character. The British Minister in China, Sir Miles Lampson, and the Foreign Secretary, Sir Austen Chamberlain, exchanged letters on the

---

York, 1925), p. 29. J. W. Bennett's novels *The Yellow Corsair* (London, 1928) and *Son of the Typhoon* (London, 1929) were quite typical in the mixing of topical plot themes — the Shaji incident and the May 30th incident respectively — and portrayals of 'Yellow Peril' anti-foreign activities related to images of the Boxer rising. For a recent examination of the historiography of the movement see Paul A. Cohen, 'The Contested Past: The Boxers as History and Myth', *Journal of Asian Studies*, 51:1 (February 1992), pp. 82–113.

[1] North China Daily News, *China in Chaos* (Shanghai, 1926), p. 1; see also Rodney Gilbert in *NCH*, 16/4/27, p. 114. Drage papers, Journal 24/9/24. For an example of Nanjing's mythologisation see Nora Waln, *Within the Walls of Nanking* (London, 1928).

[2] Mr Dickinson, Tientsin British Committee of Information, Memorandum 31, 29/9/31, 'The Tientsin Resolution', SOAS, Royal Institute of International Affairs papers, Box 10.

[3] Soothill, *China and England*, pp. 32–41; Putnam Weale, *Why China*, pp. 323–32; H. G. W. Woodhead, *A Journalist in China* (London, 1934), p. 261.

lessons to be discerned for the present in the history of Sino-British relations immediately preceding the first opium war, and from the fact that Chinese civilization was 'static'. Chamberlain agreed with Lampson that

> those vexatious anti-foreign practices which were stopped by the treaties of last century would re-appear in all their virulence if the restraining influence of the treaties was too suddenly removed.

Lampson held that the problems stemmed from the 'racial characteristics of the Chinese governing classes'.[1] Arthur H. Smith's 1892 *Chinese Characteristics*, which was also predicated on a static view of the Chinese character, was still, in the 1920s, a good seller and widely recommended reading.[2]

It has recently been pointed out how the immediately posthumous missionary discourse on the Boxer rising often equated it with the 1857 Sepoy Mutiny.[3] The comparison was widely used. In the 1920s visitors to the British Legation compound were shown a 'Lest We Forget' wall with genuine bullet holes from the siege (which still existed in 1950), or the Water Gate through which the allied troops entered the city.[4] Both of these routines were conscious recreations in the mode of memorials in India.[5]

The association with the Mutiny was not, however, only made in relation to the Boxers. 'One thought instinctively of Lucknow' wrote Naval Chaplain Scott when he saw Chongqing's Asiatic Petroleum Company installation besieged by Chinese troops but flying the Union Jack in 1926. Scott was not alone in using the Lucknow simile; Louise Jordan Miln's authorial voice used it to describe the situation in Shanghai in January 1927

[1] Lampson to Chamberlain, No. 1006, 15/9/27, FO228/3587/43 3, and Chamberlain to Lampson, 16/11/27 FO No. 1326 (F8314/2/10) FO228/3732/1 3.

[2] On the persistence of Smith's book see Bickers, 'Changing British Attitudes', pp. 30–31. See also C. W. Hayford, 'Arthur H. Smith and his China Book', in S. W. Barnett and J. K. Fairbank, eds., *Christianity in China: Early Protestant Missionary Writings* (Cambridge, Massachusetts, 1985), pp. 153–74.

[3] James Hevia, 'Leaving a Brand on China: Missionary Discourse in the Wake of the Boxer Movement', *Modern China*, 18:3, (July 1992), p. 322.

[4] Ann Bridge, *The Ginger Griffin* (London, 1934), p. 49; Daniele Varé, *The Last of the Empresses: and the Passing from the Old China to the New* (London, 1936 [1938 edition]), pp. 218–19. For information about the debate within the British embassy in 1950 about the 'Lest We Forget' wall, which then still survived, I am indebted to Mr. Derek Bryan.

[5] On the Indian model see Bernard S. Cohn, 'Representing Authority in Victorian India', in E. J. Hobsbawm and Terence Ranger, eds., *The Invention of Tradition* (Cambridge, 1983), pp. 178–79, and Charles Allen, *Plain Tales from the Raj: Images of British India in the Twentieth Century* (London, 1975), p. 57.

as the Northern Expedition neared the city.[1] Nor was the association of violence in China with that in India restricted to the previous century. The Amritsar Massacre and the shootings on May 30th 1925 in Shanghai were often compared; by critics but also by supporters of the police action that day. General Dyer's ruthlessness in India, which was largely acquitted in the court of British colonial and public opinion, as being absolutely necessary, was a precedent pointed to by those who felt the SMP had nothing to apologize for.[2]

These historical associations took place in the context of the colonial self-image of the British in China: Lucknow was certainly one of the great clichés of the British imperial story by this point but its use indicates how many Britons looked at the situation both in the treaty ports and also outside them in what was, let us not forget, independent and un-colonised China. It is also as well to remember that many of the social and business structures of the Raj were carted off to China; this even included the vocabulary of British India: tiffin, lakh, shroff, godown, coolie, bund, boy, chit.[3] Sikh policemen were used in the British concession in Hankou and in the British dominated Shanghai International Settlement (it was a detachment of Sikhs who were ordered to open fire in 1925).

IMPERIAL PRESTIGE

The underlying factor behind this choice of historical references was that the treaty port British saw themselves as constituting a colonial society. The maintenance of this colonialism lay in the protection of their prestige in China. The spectre of humiliation was an important issue. Avoidance of humiliation and maintenance of prestige were often key factors in British diplomatic tardiness and heavy-handedness.

[1] Imperial War Museum, Scott papers, Letter to his sisters, 23/10/26. 'There were Englishmen in Shanghai who thought of Lucknow,' Miln, *The Flutes of Shanghai* (London, 1928), p. 153.
[2] On comparisons with Amritsar see N. R. Clifford, *Spoilt Children of Empire: Westerners in Shanghai and the Chinese Revolution of the 1920s* (Hanover and London, 1991), p. 105. On Dyer see D. Sayer, 'British Reaction to the Amritsar Massacre 1919–1920', *Past and Present*, 131 (May 1991), pp. 130–64. The two SMP officers eventually forced to resign over the May 30th shootings received a combined annual total of £2,000 in pensions. By 1941 they had in fact received in total more than was belatedly given in compensation to relatives of the victims of the shooting in 1930, SMC, *Annual Report*, 1926–1941; Lampson to FO No. 168, 11/2/30, FO228/4132/2 2f.
[3] John Swire and Sons, Swire Archives, Oral History Transcripts, No. 5, p. 2: 'Having been in India I had an idea of what Eastern life was like'. Lionel Curtis, felt that 'The British ... are badly handicapped by traditions established in their earlier contact with India ...,' 'Notes on China', SOAS RIIA, Box 8, p. 20.

Upholding prestige involved practicalities. These included the physical structures of the British establishment in China: the gunboats,[1] control of the Customs, and the large Legation in Beijing. This 'city within a city within a city' accommodated some 2,000 people and according to one Minister: 'There is no other Legation that can compare with it; either for beauty or for dignity'.[2] The Consulates and Consulates-General throughout China fulfilled similar functions.[3] So did the foreign monuments and graveyards scattered throughout China. Reginald Johnston was worried that the return of the leased territory of Weihaiwei to China in 1930 would be followed by the destruction of British monuments and:

> the creation of a legend that the inhabitants of the Territory, having been ground under a merciless foreign yoke for over thirty years, had welcomed their liberators with tears of joy.

This was a real fear. Memorials to German rule in Qingdao were destroyed in 1930. Chinese nationalism was also sensitive about physical reminders of Western triumphs.[4]

The *Guomindang* set up their capital in Nanjing and changed Beijing's name to Beiping partly to expunge associations with the corrupt Northern governments and their subjection to the foreign powers. The British Legation remained in Beijing until 1935 and it is clear that despite the 'practical' reasons often elaborated against an earlier move the motivation was one of prestige. A new Legation would have none of the dignity nor the historical associations — of the Legation siege and the allied victory — of that in Beijing. Nanjing had also acquired humiliating overtones as a result of the Nanking Incident.[5] Furthermore, scuttling down to the Yangzi looked uncomfortably like kowtowing to a childish Nationalist whim.[6] Any

---

[1] Ichang No. 47, 2/12/30, FO228\4190\13 22r.

[2] On this perception of the Customs see FO No. 360, 8/1/30, enc. No. 2 China Confidential F6720/3/10 'British Policy in China', FO228\4134\25 3. On the Legation see Sir Owen O'Malley, *The Phantom Caravan* (London, 1954), p. 95; Lampson to Chamberlain, 9/3/27, FO800\260; the Anglophile Dutch Minister Oudendyk felt the Legation 'must make an Englishman legitimately proud of his country', *Ways and By Ways in Diplomacy* (London, 1939), p. 27.

[3] Although it was hardly dignified for the Kunming Consul-General to be living in 'a ramshackle Chinese house' leased in the name of the Governor's mistress who was trying to reclaim it, H. Phillips, 'Inspection of Yunnanfu Consulate-General', 2/3/29, FO369\2705 K5497/5497/210.

[4] Weihaiwei No. 8, 18/2/30, FO228\4253\46 51a.

[5] The temper of the times can also be gauged from the documents published in the *China Year Book*, pp. 723–36.

[6] Lampson, 'Meeting with the Spanish Ambassador', 5/7/28, FO228\3797\5 21g. The reasons spelled out in 1930 were practical ones about moving, political instability in

such concessions would only lead to 'accentuated arrogance' on the part of the Chinese, as was the result, it was claimed, of foreign representation at the State Funeral of Sun Yatsen in Nanjing in 1929.[1]

The fear of losing prestige was a recurrent theme in conservative treaty port arguments. It was entwined with notions deriving from the discourse on white race supremacy in East Asia (felt to be on the defensive after Japan's defeat of Russia in 1905)) but also sought analogies in history — Sir Miles Lampson was not alone in finding in history proof of Chinese racial characteristics.

THE USES OF HISTORY

The function of the recourse to history was mainly two-fold. Firstly it provided a focus and shape for what was otherwise a transient society — especially for those not working for the big China companies which with their own traditions and securities. There is a clearly identifiable class aspect to this — many of the most virulent users of history were lower-middle class Britons working in treaty port service sectors whose livelihoods depended on the perpetuation of the concessions and extraterritoriality. A company like Jardines, however, provided its employees with its own history and legends, even, in Shanghai, its own war memorial and its own Armistice Day ceremony.[2] Employees of such companies were perhaps more likely to identify in the first instance with the company then with the treaty port communities.

It must not be forgotten that the foreign community was subject to a steady turnover in its constituent population as older residents retired and younger men arrived (it was, overwhelmingly, a male society). It was as necessary then for *Oriental Affairs* to remind such new arrivals in 1938 of what happened 'When China Went Red', during the period of Soviet-*Guomindang*

Central China and the heat in Nanjing, 'it would clearly be mad to think of it yet', wrote Lampson to the Foreign Office, No. 143, 27/5/30, FO228\4135\1 3f. On the issue of the change from Beijing to Beiping, although approval was given for the use of 'Peiping' instead of 'Peking' in local communications, few consuls seem to have done so with any consistency. The Foreign Office did not intend, at that point, to use the name when communicating with the Chinese Legation in London, Orde to Lampson, FO No. 1169, 16/12/29, FO228\4169\1 13g.

[1] See Lampson's paraphrase of the analysis of U. S. Consul Price, to FO No. 113, 24/6/29, FO228\3937/420.

[2] *NCH*, 17/11/28, p. 253.

cooperation in the 1920s, as it was to instil the tenets of the longer-term treaty port history.[1]

Secondly, it gave a sense of historical legitimacy to defenders of the Western communities. A community with a history is a real community. The vision of treaty port history which stressed the ascendancy of Western contributions and the haughty, cruel actions of the Chinese gave treaty port Britons something to fight for that, transparently, was not just the reactionary self-interest that domestic opinion tarred them with — famously summed up by Arthur Ransome as the 'Shanghai Mind'.[2] To this purpose modern legends continued to be made: it was claimed that the Foreign Office had betrayed the treaty port British, especially over the Nationalist seizure of the British concession Hankou in January 1927; mission educationalists had 'bolshevised' China's students; the Nanjing incident was described as a planned Nationalist trial for the attack on Shanghai. These legends had the function of uniting the community against hostile outsiders, or those it felt endangered the 'good old China': Whitehall, foreign liberals, the *Guomindang*, and especially against the Chinese in general. They also represented a convenient simplification of recent political history for new arrivals to learn. It is clear that they did so.[3]

ECHOES OF THE MACARTNEY EMBASSY

It comes as no surprise to find that the Macartney mission was allotted its place in the repertoire of historical examples and moral tales. The influential Shanghai journalist Rodney Gilbert, for example, declared in 1929 that the Macartney Embassy did more harm than good and succeeded only in enrolling 'Great Britain among the tribute-bearing appendages of the Manchu throne' and fuelling the arrogance and truculence of Chinese officialdom.[4] The stigma of the *koutou*, whether technical or metaphorical, remained. Sir Frederick Maze was vilified in the treaty port press for swearing an oath of loyalty to the Guomindang and to Sun Yatsen's *sanminzhuyi* ['three principles of the people'] and also bowing his head to a portrait of Sun on his inauguration as Inspector-General of the Chinese

[1] *Oriental Affairs*, August 1938, pp. 82–86.
[2] Arthur Ransome, *The Chinese Puzzle* (London, 1927), pp. 28–32. On the question of the bad public image of the foreign community in China see my *Changing Shanghai's 'Mind': Publicity, Reform and the British in Shanghai, 1927–1931* (London, 1992), pp. 1–4, 17–18.
[3] See, for example, J. O. P. Bland on the 'Foreign Office School of Thought', *China: The Pity of It* (London, 1932), pp. 176–97. For a contemporary attempt at debunking the Nanjing rape-myths see *China Weekly Review*, 28/5/27, p. 342.
[4] *The Unequal Treaties: China and the Foreigner* (London, 1929), p. 81.

Maritime Customs in 1929.[1] More interestingly, in 1930 the ratepayers annual meeting of the Shanghai Municipal Council was roused by a British lawyer into overthrowing what was planned by its proposers to be a rubber-stamp motion to increase Chinese representation on the Council, causing a minor crisis. The lawyer declared that passing 'this resolution ... would appear to be an act of fawning sycophancy ... they will not thank you if you pass it. They will only laugh at your weakness and your folly'. To back up his argument he finished with a sizeable quotation from Qianlong's letter to George III as proof of the characteristic hostility and arrogance of the Chinese to foreigners, concluding that this 'spirit in its undiluted form is still to be found in many influential circles in China today'.[2]

The implications of this use of history for British reactions to the rise of nationalism in 1920s China were tangible. It fuelled the conservatism of treaty port reactions, coloured the tutelary and dismissive vocabulary of British businessmen and the underscored the pervasive sense of friendship spurned and guardianship wronged. Britain's retreat from China in the 1920s and 1930s was a stubborn, slow and bad-tempered affair. In times of heightened tension the language resorted to by those under threat was often colourful and usually extreme, and perhaps unrelated to more sober thinking. On that basis it is tempting to downplay the importance of the themes to be found. However, it is more likely to be the case that concepts resorted to *in extremis* reflect more closely the tangible beliefs of their articulators. They certainly reveal the strength of the socialisation process in the treaty port communities.

This paper has been concerned with the treaty port communities and their defenders in a period when they felt equally threatened by Chinese nationalism and changes in Britain's policy towards China. It highlights a trend that did not begin in this period, nor end with it. It is clear that the most important work had yet to be done. The real turning point came with the years of tension before Pearl Harbour. Many treaty port Britons initially saw in Japan's actions in China after 1931 a vindication of their own conservatism and imperialism, and an accomplishment of their own desires. As tensions with the Japanese were heightened — notably during the Tianjin dispute and in the politics of the Shanghai International Settlement between 1939 and 1941 — British perceptions shifted. The Chinese became British allies. The initially pro-Japanese political lobby, the British Residents' Association, became a community support organisation after

[1] Bickers, 'Changing British Attitudes', p. 106.
[2] *NCH*, 22/4/30, p. 148.

December 7th 1941.[1] For British residents internment by the Japanese appeared to have wiped away memories of the pre-war atmosphere and dominant attitudes. Halcyon days of Sino-British cooperation and joint opposition to the Japanese menace stretched back endlessly from 1941.

[1] Bickers, 'Changing British Attitudes', pp. 164–66, 247, 248.

Notes on Contributors

P. J. MARSHALL is Rhodes Professor of Imperial History at Kings College, London. He is the author of numerous articles, and longer works such as *The British Discovery of Hinduism in the Eighteenth Century* (1970), *East Indian Fortunes* (1976), *Bengal: The British Bridgehead* (1987). He is also joint editor, with Glyndwr Williams, of *The Great Map of Mankind: British Perceptions of the World in the Age of Enlightenment* (1982).

ZHANG SHUNHONG is a research fellow at the Institute of World History, Chinese Academy of Social Sciences, Beijing, having completed his doctoral dissertation, on contemporary British views of China during the Macartney and Amherst Missions, at Birkbeck College, London in 1990.

JAMES L. HEVIA is Professor of History at the North Carolina Agricultural and Technical State University, Greensboro, North Carolina. Author of numerous articles on the theme of this book, its implications and resonances, he is currently working on a monograph concerned with the Macartney mission.

WANG TSENG-TSAI is Professor of History at the National Taiwan University, Taipei, Taiwan. An expert on Qing diplomatic history, his publications include *Collected Essays on Late Ch'ing Diplomacy* (1978) and *Collected Essays on Sino-British Relations* (1983).

ROBERT A. BICKERS recently completed his doctorate at the School of Oriental and African Studies, University of London, and will shortly take up a junior research fellowship at Nuffield College, Oxford, specialising in the history of treaty port institutions in China from 1843 to 1943.